Kilimanjaro Unfiltered

KILIMANJARO
UNFILTERED

DANICA PAIGE

THE REAL, RAW, RUGGED TRUTH OF SUMMITING
THE WORLD'S TALLEST FREESTANDING
MOUNTAIN

TO EVERYONE WHO DONATED toward my Kilimanjaro Challenge! As you'll learn in the journey ahead, climbing Mount Kilimanjaro was just half of my adventure. The challenge also consisted of raising 5,000 euros (5,422 dollars) to support marginalized youth in Kenya. Without you, I couldn't have made this trip happen, and more importantly, we couldn't have made such an amazing impact in the lives of these young people. Thank you from the bottom of my heart.

CONTENTS

THE IDEA

HAVE YOU EVER WOKEN up one morning and thought, "Climbing Mount Kilimanjaro sounds like fun"? Yeah … me neither! After learning that there was an opportunity to climb Mount Kilimanjaro with some of my colleagues from around the globe, I slowly started believing it sounded fun!

Even crazier, I figured that climbing Mount Kilimanjaro would be one of the most challenging things I've done in my life. So, on June 17, 2023, I decided that I wanted to write a book about it!

And that's exactly what I have done. *Kilimanjaro Unfiltered* will be exactly that: *unfiltered*. In a world full of social media, where everyone puts a filter on everything, I'm breaking the mold. Throughout this expedition, I'll lay bare my raw and genuine perspectives and experiences. Strap in! It's bound to be a bumpy ride!

As you delve into *Kilimanjaro Unfiltered*, you'll gain a comprehensive understanding of how this adventure began and everything that went into preparing for it. From detailed cost breakdowns and essential packing lists to an account of my chaotic flight experience and a day-by-day overview of the climb, this book covers it all. By the end, you'll have a clear sense of what it takes to reach the summit. Whether you're inspired to take on Kilimanjaro yourself or are encouraged to pursue a different challenge, my hope is that my journey motivates you to step outside your comfort zone. After all, the best stories often start with doing something you never imagined you could.

Given the unfiltered nature of this content, proceed at your own discretion. While not inappropriate, the book is a reflection of my own opinions, and I won't shy away from punctuating a few sentences with emphatic f-bombs to convey my true feelings and emotions. Consider yourself warned! And, lastly, all characters have been given aliases to protect their true identities. I've selected Swahili names as the main language in Tanzania is Swahili.

THE BEGINNING

IT'S 2023. THE WORLD has undergone significant transformations over the last three years. My passion for travel, unwavering commitment to fitness, and competitive spirit have remained constants, however. The thrill of tackling challenges fuels my curiosity.

It all started in February of 2023 with a post on our internal company website that was titled "Kilimanjaro Challenge." In truth, credit goes to one of my closest friends and colleagues, Zuri, who graciously shared the link with me. Upon learning about the challenge she'd signed up for, I was overcome with a blend of jealousy and the fear of missing out. Without hesitation, I submitted my application.

You may wonder why I even considered this endeavor in the first place. I've always been known to travel at a moment's notice, participate in fitness challenges, and experience new things. When I learned about Kilimanjaro, it checked a lot of my boxes and instantly aligned with my spontaneity. One time, I even spontaneously decided to fly from Florida to Utah to run a marathon with no formal training. (By the way, I *hate* running!) As it turned out, that was a terrible idea. I managed to complete twenty-two of the twenty-six miles, but the excruciating pain in my foot prevented me from formally crossing the finish line. Although defeating, that spontaneous marathon gave me a whole new level of appreciation for marathon runners. So have no doubt; you won't need to be a runner to climb this mountain, that is certain! But it won't hurt if you are an avid runner, of course.

I am also extremely passionate about travel and will use any excuse I can to leave home. I started traveling out of the country in 2018, and since then, I've visited over twenty countries. My friend Zuri has also been my travel partner in crime for many of those trips, so the fact that she was going to participate in the challenge too gave me some peace of mind. We are definitely the type of friends that call each other and say, "Hey, do you want to go to Africa on Friday?" It's become a common joke among my friends, and now everyone always asks, "Where are you off to next?" instead of asking how I'm doing or what is new. With the excitement and opportunity to travel to three new countries, along with the physical challenge, I thought to myself, "Why not?" I definitely wanted to try something new!

Yet this was no ordinary challenge. A mere twenty individuals would be selected, and we would all shoulder the responsibility of raising 5,000 euros (5,422 dollars)—a financial commitment that added a layer of complexity to an already daunting endeavor. However, the donations we would raise would support a great cause, which continued to add to my inspiration for applying to the Kilimanjaro Challenge! Specifically, our donations would be invested in enhancing the livelihoods and well-being of one hundred young, marginalized women (aged eighteen to thirty-five) in Nairobi, Kenya, through decent jobs. I'll touch more on what that means soon.

Unfortunately, my initial application faced rejection, and I accepted it as a twist of fate, a missed opportunity. Little did I know that destiny had other plans for me. Thirteen days later (on February 22, 2023), a serendipitous turn of events unfolded when a slot opened, and I found myself next in line on the waiting list. The question posted in the email echoed in my mind: was I still interested? Without a moment's hesitation, I thought, "Duh, absolutely!"

And so the enchanting chapter of this adventure commenced. The anticipation and thrill of orchestrating the trip, coupled with the challenge of fundraising over the ensuing months, became the focal points of my existence. What I haven't told you yet is what I do for a living. I am a certified project management professional (PMP), and I direct a team of project managers while also continuing to manage projects myself. While I spend all day being a project manager, I still wear the PM hat in my personal life. It's definitely a lifestyle and is ingrained in my blood. I revel in creating checklists, drafting schedules, and immersing myself in all the details. At this juncture, I was unabashedly nerding out over the prospect of what lay ahead.

Navigating the preparations for Kilimanjaro stirred a whirlwind of inquiries in my mind. How does one get themselves physically fit for such an endeavor? Is there a specific training regimen that I would need to follow? What attire is deemed essential? And what shopping list must I compile? Amid the whirlwind, my personal life was bustling with its own activity, but the prospect of staying occupied invigorated me. This challenge held immense significance, and I was resolute in surmounting any impediments that might cross my path.

As the multitude of questions swirled within my mind, they naturally coalesced into distinct categories demanding my attention: philanthropy, preparation, and packing. An unforeseen and unintentional alliteration emerged, which I have affectionately dubbed the 3P's!

Philanthropy

Working for the world's largest HR services company opens doors to a plethora of global programs, and one of our impactful initiatives involved partnering with Voluntary Services Overseas (VSO). In 2023, the team opted for a remarkable challenge, as you have already come to learn: scaling Mount Kilimanjaro. The fundraising efforts were pretty significant, and with twenty participants each raising 5,000 euros (or 5,422 dollars), we were destined to raise over 100,000 euros (or 108,440 dollars) collectively. The expectation was for us to reach one hundred women through our contributions.

I felt connected to the mission of women empowerment, which fueled my desire to help. I have always felt that I was forced to be independent at a young age due to my parents' divorce. This sparked the necessity to do things on my own, like doing my own laundry, for instance. It may seem simple, but no twelve-year-old really enjoys taking on those "adulting" tasks at such a young age. Looking back, it made me fiercely strong and independent. Knowing that the donations would allow young women to be more independent really resonated with me.

To achieve all of these ambitions, the VSO group aimed to provide training, financial services, market access, and quality assurance, in addition to fostering partnerships with service providers to ensure sustainable development and gender equality in the blue economy sector. In turn, this would allow them to provide childcare assistance, as many of the women were single mothers, which often prevented them from working and thus earning an income. I loved learning all the details behind how my funds would support others. This was also critical as I began to ponder how I would raise money.

Now, I must confess, the realm of fundraising was foreign territory for me. I'd never dabbled in the art of Girl Scouts and those elementary school fundraisers. Let's just say I had a knack for conveniently sidestepping them. But, with my outgoing nature, I thought, "How hard could it be?" Well, let's just say I was in for a reality check. (Note to my dad: if you're reading this, feel free to frame and hang this page on the wall, highlighting the admission of being wrong. I'm a work in progress, OK?)

As I was figuring out how to promote the Kilimanjaro Challenge and our partnership with VSO, I envisioned crafting an informational video. During my undergraduate studies, I'd majored in marketing and always thought that I would end up in a marketing career. As you've found out, I somehow landed in the project management space, but I do still try to leverage my marketing knowledge in this digital age. However, I will admit that content creation isn't really my forte. It seems as if all the Gen Z kids have that specialty. Or the professionals.

That's where my friend Hadithi comes into the picture. I reached out to him on Instagram because I was aware of his skills in crafting gym videos with voice-overs. To my delight, he generously volunteered his services. I will forever be grateful, and it turned out to be an incredibly fun, and sometimes challenging, experience! I particularly wanted to create a video that included me working out, to demonstrate that this was going to be a physical challenge. While I wanted it to be a way to introduce all aspects of the challenge, it was important that it showcased my *why*.

In April, the official collaboration kicked off with a bang. Our video shoot unfolded over two sessions. On one occasion, Hadithi joined me at the gym, and I powered through the programmed workout of the day (WOD), courtesy of CrossFit. (Thank you, CrossFit magic!) About a week later, the scene shifted to my living room as Hadithi skillfully set up his camera. Yes, it was interview time! Armed with a vague notion of what I wanted to convey about my impending Kilimanjaro climb and the accompanying challenge of fundraising for underprivileged youth in Kenya, I dived into the initial videos. To put it mildly, they were all trash! I was racing through my words, veering off-topic, avoiding eye contact with the camera—essentially, a recipe for disaster. Fortunately, Hadithi being the seasoned professional he is, stepped in and suggested, "Let's write a script." I rolled my eyes and protested; after all, my aim was authenticity, not robotic recitation. After numerous script iterations, we finally struck gold. The script, penned on good, old-fashioned computer paper (if people still call it that!), became our secret sauce. Hadithi held the pages under the lens for me to read, ensuring I maintained a connection with the camera. Authenticity was the key, scripted or not, and I think we nailed it. I may be biased.

Imagine me sitting in my living room in a teal swivel chair, with a collection of photos from my travels on the wall behind me. I call this my travel wall, and I will continue to add photos and memories as I increase the number of countries I travel to. The camera starts rolling, and I begin to introduce myself and the VSO organization. I explain that I will be raising donations for marginalized young women and training to climb Mount Kilimanjaro in the future months. The video frequently pans from my living room to my local CrossFit gym. (I wanted to pair the storytelling with also capturing the action, including the physical training aspect.)

I go on to explain that my motivation for this challenge is deeply personal—many people in my life have been affected by terminal illnesses, which robbed them of the ability to move freely. I work out every day because I can, and I never take that for granted, knowing how fortunate I am to have this capability. I've undertaken this challenge on behalf of those who can't. The video then ends with my hook to encourage people to click the link in my bio to help me reach my goal with this once-in-a-lifetime opportunity. End scene.

Fast-forward to the beginning of May, and the finished product made its grand debut across my social media landscape: LinkedIn, Instagram, and Facebook. I also took the liberty of uploading it to YouTube for direct sharing via text (a nod to my relatives without social media) and LinkedIn. Yet a significant challenge loomed: our donation platform. Working for a global company meant our website hailed from the Netherlands, hence the references to raising €5,000. Conveying this to a crowd of Americans sparked a deluge of questions: How much is that in US dollars? How can I pay? Why does the website seem sketchy? Why is my card being declined? These were but a few of the queries that flooded my inbox. To ease the confusion, I included my personal Venmo link on the donation page, allowing people to contribute in US dollars, which I would then convert and donate on their behalf. It was a makeshift solution, but it certainly helped. What did not help, however, were the exchange rates. Unfortunately, there is not a one-to-one ratio when converting US dollars to euros, so I ended up spending a lot of my own money covering the difference. As an example, in September of 2023, €20.00 was $21.69. It may not seem like a lot, but those dollars add up quickly when you're trying to raise €5,000!

Anyway, my fundraising journey unfolded predominantly on social media, with Instagram and LinkedIn taking center stage. I also reached out directly to family members and close friends. To my surprise, a considerable number of my colleagues generously contributed. Strangely, it left me somewhat vexed. Don't get me wrong; I'm profoundly grateful for their support. But ponder this: why were individuals I'd worked with for a mere three years or less more eager to donate than some people I've known my entire life, including blood relatives and friends I've unwaveringly supported? It felt like a bit of a reality check, and while I hold no lingering resentment (for the most part), I do hope that if you happen to be one of those friends in that category, you're currently engrossed in my book. In that case, consider forgiveness granted.

I understand that, in today's economy, it can feel like you barely have a few dollars to spare—especially with the soaring costs of groceries, gas, and utilities. But my fundraising journey has shown me that giving back doesn't have to be overwhelming. Sometimes, it's as simple as skipping one Starbucks trip or passing on a fast-food run to contribute to a meaningful cause. This experience has broadened my perspective, making me more empathetic and understanding when friends reach out for support in their charitable efforts.

At one juncture, I attempted to orchestrate a charity 5k walk and run event through my gym, but it didn't quite pan out. This, too, proved to be a source of frustration. I've been an avid supporter for my gym, consistently promoting them on social media with tags and shout-outs whenever the opportunity arises. Initially, the response was positive—a resounding "Yes, that sounds great!" But, as I tried to follow up and nail down a date, the whole endeavor fell through. Disheartened and uncharacteristically defeated, I threw in the towel, deeming it unworthy of further investment of my time. Despite the letdown, I still hold love for my gym fam. To those few who did contribute ... thank you; your support was truly appreciated.

Throughout the months, I maintained a consistent social media presence and reached out directly to individuals, asking if they were interested in supporting the cause. While most people responded, some chose silence. Here's the deal: I completely understand if you can't donate or aren't interested. What I can't understand is the lack of response; that's plain lazy and, dare I say, rude. I'm exhausted by the prevailing attitude in this generation that deems it acceptable to avoid responding and evade confrontation by expressing genuine feelings. It's time to stop filtering. It's as simple as saying, "Thanks for reaching out. I'll think about it and donate if it makes sense," or, "That's so cool! I can't donate, but I'll be cheering for you." Why is that so difficult? Surprisingly, three of my friends *still* haven't responded. Have I bothered to circle back with them? Absolutely not. Call me salty, but perhaps we weren't great friends from the outset. Lesson learned.

Sorry, but as promised, this is an unfiltered story. Still with me? It's remarkably liberating to speak my mind without restraint. If you could hear half the unspoken thoughts rattling around in my head, you might not be so fond of me. But, before I delve too deeply into the rabbit hole, let's bring it back to the matters that will pique your interest. I did warn you that this book would be a collection of my unfiltered opinions, and I'm not sugarcoating it for anyone.

I thought it might be helpful if I shared the context of what was in my direct text messages. Perhaps you'll have an opportunity to raise donations soon and will need a little guidance. Here's what I came up with:

Hi! It would mean a lot if you spent two minutes watching this video. I'm currently asking family and friends for donations as I take on the Mount Kilimanjaro Challenge in October with my coworkers. My donation page is also linked for more information. All donations will help young women with access to better jobs and a better quality of life. And the best part: I actually get to *see* the donations put to use as I volunteer my time after climbing the mountain. Donations are in euros and accepted via Visa/Mastercard/PayPal; sometimes you have to submit payment twice because most banks flag it as fraud with it being a Netherlands website. Or, if you prefer to donate in US dollars, I'm accepting Venmo and can donate on your behalf.

I know the message seems long for a text, but I aimed to give all the detail so people could make informed decisions. I also created a shorter version and a follow-up text.

I dedicated my time over four months to raise these donations, and if I had to give any advice, it would be to start early. In total, I successfully raised four thousand euros, personally contributing the final one thousand to meet the required threshold for participation. Closing that financial gap was a gratifying endeavor, especially considering the notable cause the funds supported: providing underprivileged young women with access to meaningful green jobs. The beneficiaries, primarily single mothers, were facing challenges in employment due to childcare affordability issues. Our collective effort would infuse them with hope and a chance at economic independence.

While my primary focus leading up to the trip was securing donations, there was still another significant task on the horizon: acquiring everything I didn't already possess. Enter the preparation phase! But, before diving into the shopping spree, I needed to take inventory of what I already had!

Preparation

You've learned that I have an unwavering commitment to fitness, and I've mentioned CrossFit. I also love boxing, biking, and really anything to keep me in physical shape. I played soccer when I was growing up, but as I've gotten older, I have realized that I can't play sports the way I used to. Considering my highly active lifestyle, my wardrobe leans heavily toward leggings and sports bras. Fun fact: I actually own over forty pairs of leggings, and they are organized by color in my closet. I even have a matching sports bra for the majority of the leggings' colors. Unfortunately, residing in sunny Florida has left my collection of cold-weather gear rather underwhelming. In fact, it's downright lacking. As I delved into the trip planning, a comprehensive list of essential items was provided from our tour company. Yes, we used a tour company to guide our trip. (By the way, it was an individual cost of $1,750 for the guide company.) In case you don't know, you can't just decide you're going to climb Mount Kilimanjaro by yourself. It requires a guide. I find this fact very interesting, and you'll come to learn later that I could have never survived this climb without a guide. Nonetheless, the list from the tour guide prompted me to assess my existing inventory and identify the considerable gaps. Spoiler alert: I needed a lot. For those who are curious or aspiring Kilimanjaro conquerors, the complete list will be tucked away in the back of the book, ready to be your guide when the time comes.

For those of you who are into horoscopes, I'm a Leo through and through. Leos are known to be bold, generous, and full of life. Leos generally have a special—even grand—view of their birthday; it's their personal "day to shine!" For me, it's my *month* to shine. I'm the kind of person who celebrates the entire month of July. So, of course, I leveraged my birthday as an opportune moment to request essential items for my upcoming adventure. After taking inventory of what I needed, I created an Amazon wish list full of essentials. I extended the invitation to family members and close friends, hoping I'd get a few things for my trip. Luckily, this tactic worked well, and I was blessed with a solar charger, a brand-new purple rain jacket, and the ultimate necessity: a sleeping bag!

Remember the good old days of camping out in the back-yard with friends, enclosed in sleeping bags? Well, let me debunk the nostalgia. It's an entirely different ball game when you're the adult. Can I just express how fucking challenging it is to stuff a sleeping bag back into its original sleeve? It's practically a standalone workout. I found myself resorting to YouTube tutorials, desperately trying to master the art of folding and rolling while exerting enough force to keep it tight. The struggle became real, and I'm extremely grateful for the practice rounds at home. Just envision the potential disaster if I had attempted this spectacle for the first time in front of an audience. Now I proudly proclaim myself a pro in the fine art of repacking a sleeping bag into its original case!

In the realm of preparations, beyond the thoughtful birthday gifts I received, a crucial item still lingered on my checklist: a day pack. After careful consideration, I opted for the practicality of a twenty-five-liter WOLFpak book bag, steering clear of the conventional hiking bags. My rationale extended beyond the immediate needs of the trek; I sought a companion that would seamlessly integrate into my posthike lifestyle. The chosen bag, adored with stylish black and hot-pink zippers and accents, subtly persuaded me into the purchase. I also really liked the variety of compartments, which was sure to keep me organized. Hello, I'm a project manager! I love organization, of course. The internal debate between a twenty-five-liter and a thirty-five-liter bag raged on within me, and ultimately, I found peace in the decision to embrace the smaller but more efficient option. From a logical perspective, a larger bag would equate to more storage, translating to a heftier load on my back. I added the twenty-five-liter backpack to my virtual shopping cart for a cost of $125, and I eagerly anticipated the bag's arrival, fueling my excitement for the impending adventure. There were also pink shaker bottles that matched the bag, so I was convinced I needed two of them! Yet a lingering question remained: what about everything else I needed?

While embarking on this journey, remaining cost-consciousness became my steadfast approach. In the pursuit of frugality, I meticulously scoured for deals to ensure I spent judiciously. For my essential cold-weather gear, I strategically made my way to the Columbia outlet store, opting for a series of visits to distribute the expenses. Admittedly, the total expenditure remained constant, yet I've always adhered to the philosophy of numerous modest transactions rather than a single substantial one. This tactical approach somehow assuages my financial sensibilities. Some may even call it girl math!

The initial visits focused on securing foundational items: hiking boots, hiking socks, and long-sleeve dry-fit shirts. My hiking boots were around $70 at the outlet store, but the socks cost $10–15 per pair, and I ended up with six (one for each day of the climb). The long-sleeve dry-fit shirts were $20 each, and I got two of those. I probably visited three or four times before securing all nine of those items. I made frequent visits and waited for sales! During the grand-finale shopping spree, I splurged and spent $269.14. This expenditure encompassed a comprehensive array of items including thermal pants, a thermal long-sleeve shirt, a fleece pullover, ski pants, and the crown jewel: my summit jacket. Notably, the standout steal was my down jacket, a serendipitous find that had been marked down from $150 to a mere $54.98. Its fortuitous match with the available ski pants was an added bonus. My love affair with outlet shopping, where quality meets affordability, was profoundly reaffirmed. Sharing the nitty-gritty of my expenses is not just transparency but also a genuine attempt to set a realistic financial expectation for anyone contemplating the allure of scaling Kilimanjaro. If you already live in a cold place, you may be at an advantage with existing gear. I spent nearly $500 on clothes and accessories.

Beyond the clothing, there were essential accessories required, for which Walmart and Amazon emerged as the prime enablers. No shocker there. As promised, the exhaustive packing list, complete with all the nitty-gritty essentials, awaits you at the conclusion of this book. Feel free to fast-track your journey straight to the goods, if that's your true area of interest.

It's crucial to recognize that considerations extend beyond material items like clothes and accessories. Often overlooked are the essential aspects of required and recommended vaccines and medications, particularly when venturing into a third-world country. While having an established primary care doctor would have been convenient, I leveraged modern technology to find a suitable travel health doctor online. The consultation, spanning twenty minutes, came with a hefty price tag of one hundred dollars.

While it's true that if your travel route takes you only from the US to Tanzania, vaccines may not be mandatory, my plan to visit Kenya necessitated the vaccine for yellow fever. Opting for convenience, I paid $300 for the vaccine, potentially missing out on a more economical option elsewhere. Additionally, antimalarial pills, strongly recommended for the region, were offered at $8 per pill during the travel doctor's visit, totaling $176 for the required twenty-two pills. I thought to myself, "Fuck that!" Refusing to succumb to these extreme costs, I requested a prescription instead.

In a stroke of serendipity, my local pharmacy proved to be a beacon of affordability, filling the prescription for a mere twelve dollars. The encounter was further enriched by the pharmacy tech's Kilimanjaro roots, leading to valuable food recommendations. Reflecting on the experience, I acknowledge that seeking elsewhere for the yellow fever vaccine might have saved me some money. Nevertheless, every aspect of the journey, including the unexpected connections, became an integral part of the adventure.

Alright … with my donation strategy in place and the necessary items for packing identified, I still had the training plan to map out, the booking of flights, and the actual packing before I could confidently declare myself ready for this adventure! Who knew there would be so much planning?

As a frequent traveler, I rely on a few go-to websites and apps to find the best flight deals. For this trip, I used a combination of resources, including my favorite app, Hopper, along with the trusty Google search, which ultimately led me to the best deal.

If you haven't tried Hopper yet, this is my shameless plug to download it. One of its standout features is the red/yellow/green pricing heat map, which shows the cheapest days to fly to your destination based on your preferred date range. For instance, if you're planning a trip from Orlando to London, Hopper will highlight the most affordable travel days over the coming months. This tool is incredibly useful if your travel dates are flexible. It also gives you a heads-up on when to buy your tickets, advising whether you should book now or wait, and what price trends you can expect.

A self-proclaimed travel enthusiast, I pride myself on finding the best flight deals. I booked my flight to Tanzania through justfly.com, and it was around $850 one way. I booked my flight home separately because I would be leaving from Nairobi, Kenya. I booked that flight through my CapitalOne credit card account so I could use some of my points, but it was still $750 for that flight. I booked my flights in early July, about two months ahead of the departure. In a later chapter, I'll dive into my entire flight journey, detailing the route and much more.

A frequently asked question is, "How did you train for the climb?" While I'd love to claim a meticulously crafted training plan, the reality was quite different. My usual workout routine involves CrossFit five times a week, so I predominantly stuck to that regimen. Occasionally, I'd venture to a conventional gym for a StairMaster workout, but I can count those instances on one hand. Throughout my research, a recurring piece of advice emphasized the importance of breaking in my hiking boots. I dedicated a significant amount of time (four months prior) to this task and incorporated walks with a 14-pound (6.35-kilogram) weighted vest to simulate carrying a backpack. Reflecting on the experience, focusing more on this aspect would have been beneficial.

Living in Florida, where the terrain is predominantly flat, presented a unique challenge. While I could walk for hours, it didn't adequately prepare me for the uphill climbs. Luckily, before learning about Kilimanjaro, I had planned a summer trip to Alaska—a perfect opportunity for hiking. My childhood best friend had moved to Alaska ten years prior, and I'd never gone to visit. My visit was long overdue, but also very timely. During an eight-hour layover in Seattle on my way to Alaska, I rented a car and drove to Snow Lake. The breathtaking five-mile hike to an alpine lake, my first of its kind, took approximately three hours. However, the aftermath was unexpected; I couldn't walk for two days because my calves had tightened up. I'll blame it on the airplanes.

After recovering from the soreness of my Seattle hike, I felt primed to take on a genuine Alaskan trek. A Google search led me to the Reed Lakes Trail, promising alpine lake views akin to the stunning scenes in Seattle. Convinced this was the perfect preparation for Kilimanjaro, I embarked on the journey, intentionally going solo to acclimate to the backpack I'd wear for the African summit. The pack felt light and manageable, but I'd grossly underestimated the trail's challenges. With no cell service, the hike was serene yet posed risks of encountering bears or losing my way. One of these fears materialized.

While navigating the trail, I reached the first alpine lake, meeting two fellow hikers whom I gladly offered to photograph. Reciprocating, they convinced me to continue to the second lake—a decision I initially resisted but now appreciate for the breathtaking views. At the second lake, I made another trail companion and exchanged photo duties. Lesson learned: if you want a picture, just ask! As I retraced my steps, a sense of unease settled in. Suddenly, I found myself on a set of boulders, eerily familiar from the ascent but seemingly leading toward uncertainty. Panic set in as I felt isolated with no one in sight. Trusting my instincts, I decided to climb the rocks back up, desperately seeking familiar terrain. It genuinely felt like the scene of a thriller movie.

My anxious climb was interrupted by the sound of voices. Two girls with a dog emerged, heading toward the trailhead. I yelled out, confirming they were indeed on the path heading back to the start. Gratefully, I followed them until I safely rejoined the trail. While getting lost mid-hike is far from ideal, my sense of direction and ability to heed my instincts proved invaluable. The Alaskan adventure turned out to be a ten-mile journey, unexpectedly becoming the most relative training for Kilimanjaro. Those boulders, despite momentarily leading me astray, unwittingly prepared me for the challenges of summit night.

Upon my return from Alaska, I found myself with just under a month before the official commencement of the Kilimanjaro journey. Now, let's fast-forward to one week before the big adventure. The excitement was building, and the reality of the impending challenge was sinking in. However, my enthusiasm took an unexpected hit when, out of the blue, I lost all my energy and felt like I'd been hit by a truck. The realization hit me: I was sick. Waking up with a fever, I knew I needed to prioritize rest if I stood any chance of making it to Kilimanjaro. Opting for half days at work, I dedicated myself to getting ample sleep and hydration, determined to bounce back.

Despite battling illness, I still faced a crucial decision: whether to take Diamox. The pro of taking the pill was that it would potentially help alleviate symptoms of altitude sickness. The con was that I could have a bad reaction to the drug. I was scared to take a chance on a medication I had never taken before. The choice weighed on me until the last minute, but I ultimately decided it was worth trying. A quick and easy phone call with a virtual doctor resulted in a prescription for twenty pills, setting me back a mere nine dollars. As the week progressed, my health took a positive turn, reinforcing the importance of heeding the messages from one's body and making informed decisions for the journey ahead.

Packing

The packing process, no joke, was a downright nightmare. Questions flooded my mind: Do I have too much? Did I forget something crucial? What goes in my day pack versus my duffel bag? And how on earth do I keep the duffel bag under 35 pounds (15.88 kilograms)? Why 35 pounds, you may ask? There is indeed a weight limit on the bag you can bring up the mountain. After all, I don't think anyone is interested in carrying something heavier than that up the tallest freestanding mountain in the world! Anyway, enter the project manager in me—I had a solution up my sleeve. Can you guess what it was? A project plan, of course! I meticulously crafted a plan, mapping out each day and the corresponding clothing requirements. Simultaneously, I maintained a separate checklist encompassing all the nonclothing essentials. Throughout the packing ordeal, I relied on both my project plan and my checklist to ensure nothing was left behind. I broke it down into two major components: suitcase versus carry-on (my day pack).

Just three days before my departure, I decided to revamp my entire packing strategy after hearing about my colleagues' plans. So off I went to buy new luggage—just when I'd thought my shopping sprees were over. However, fate had a stylish twist in store for me. I stumbled upon a twenty-eight-inch hot-pink suitcase for forty dollars at Marshalls that perfectly matched the pink on my day pack. It was too tempting to resist. Learning that we could store our luggage at a hotel during our mountain climb was a game changer. Now I could stow my empty duffel bag inside my suitcase, along with all the essentials for Kenya. The shift from squeezing everything into a thirty-five-pound duffel bag to having an extra fifteen pounds in a spacious suitcase (since a checked bag can weigh up to fifty pounds) felt like a woman's dream come true in this situation!

The night before my flight, I meticulously double-checked my packing list over and over, driven by the anxiety of forgetting something essential. One of my main concerns was the possibility of mosquito bites, especially since we had been instructed to take antimalarial pills. Being someone who mosquitoes seem to target relentlessly—often leaving me with itchy, swollen bites—I felt I needed to be extra cautious. During my research, I came across a product called Permethrin, an insect repellent that can be sprayed on clothing and is said to last through up to six washes. For about fifteen dollars at Walmart, I picked up a twenty-four-ounce bottle and treated all the clothes I planned to wear during the trek, hoping it would be a solid precaution. In hindsight, though, I'm not sure it was necessary.

As I continued to pack, to quell any lingering doubts, I snapped pictures of the contents as a fail-safe. Taking technology into my hands, I also equipped my luggage with an AirTag for added security, especially since this trip demanded checking a bag. I don't normally check a bag because of the added trip time. No, thank you! Only after ensuring that every essential was neatly stowed did I ceremoniously zip up my luggage, allowing the full weight of excitement to settle in.

THE FLIGHT JOURNEY

EMBARKING ON MY JOURNEY, fate decided to throw a curveball when my period started the night before my travels. Apologies to my male audience; I won't dwell on it. I was already dreading the long flight, and now I had this obstacle to deal with. Wonder-fucking-ful. Let's toss in a bit more to my already overflowing bags. No big deal. Being a woman can be so taxing. For the record, women, even if you aren't expecting your period, you should 100 percent prepare, because altitude is actually known to trigger your cycle, and you never know how your body might react up there. If you're just reading to learn about my journey and have no desire to climb the mountain, that's totally fine, too, and I appreciate your company!

Anyway, the time came, and everything was packed and ready! It was Friday afternoon. I worked until about 3:00 p.m., and then it was time to head to the airport! But first, what would be my final meal in the states before I left? Come on … this is an important debate. I settled on my favorite Mexican restaurant and ordered my usual. My meal of choice is chicken-and-spinach enchiladas with rice and beans. Spoiler alert: it did not disappoint. With a satisfied belly, I made my way to the airport.

The journey to Kilimanjaro was an adventure itself, with no direct flights from the United States. Three flights awaited me, totaling a thirty-hour journey, including flight times and layovers. Talk about exhausting. If you're fortunate enough for first-class luxury, envy ensured; I, however, couldn't drop ten grand on such opulence.

My first flight was a quick thirty-seven minutes from Orlando to Miami. Navigating the massive Miami International Airport to reach my new gate proved to be a time-consuming challenge. No moving walkways or trains to speed up the process … disappointing. It took me thirty minutes to walk there. I also had to transfer my boarding pass once I got to the gate because I'd started with American Airlines (for the domestic flight) and the international flights were through their sister airline, Qatar Airways. It took about fifteen extra minutes to wait in line for that. When I got to the counter, the gate agent asked if I had any luggage, and I provided the luggage tag receipt from the previous flight. Good thing I'd held on to that! I finally got on the plane and settled in for my fifteen-hour flight to Doha, Qatar. Are you good with geography? I'll help spell it out for you: Qatar is technically in the Middle East. Apparently, it makes more sense to fly past Africa on the way to Africa. Unbelievable.

Surviving the long fifteen-hour flight solo involved a combination of Netflix shows, in-flight movies, and strategic naps. A ten-dollar investment in internet access satisfied my scrolling fix. An aisle seat, my trusty inflatable travel pillow, and coping with Mother Nature's untimely gift kept me going. By the way, I'll never take another flight that's longer than four hours without bringing my inflatable travel pillow. It's an absolute game changer. Remember sleeping with your head on the desk in elementary school? It's like that, but ten times more comfortable.

I landed in Doha, and my next mission was to find Zuri, who was traveling from Minnesota, and another coworker named Amani, whom we had yet to meet, traveling from Canada. We had arranged ahead of time to have our flights arrive around the same time so that we could enjoy our nine-hour layover together. I was able to connect to the airport's Wi-Fi upon landing and was quickly able to find Amani! We immediately hugged and began chatting as we ventured to find Zuri. The Doha airport was massive. There were so many shopping options and food options, and the signage was not helping us find Zuri very easily. After what felt like a wild goose chase, we finally found her! Success!

Through our pretravel interactions, we learned that a total of seven of us would have layovers in Doha. Our plan was to venture beyond the airport and connect with and meet those fellow hikers. However, what began as a promising layover took a disconcerting turn when the customs line stretched to an agonizing two-hour wait. This marked the onset of my apprehension; not due to the prolonged customs ordeal, but because my AirTag indicated that my bag was still languishing in Miami. Initially, I clung on to the hope that it was a mere glitch, reassuring myself that the tracking technology had simply failed to update. "It must be here," I thought optimistically. Yet my anxiety grew as both Zuri and Amani received timely updates from their AirTags, confirming their bags' presence in Doha. Despite my concerns, I endeavored to remain composed, desperately crossing my fingers (and toes) that it was indeed a technological hiccup, and that my baggage would miraculously rejoin me in Tanzania!

After finally getting out of the Doha airport, we drove over to the downtown area to see the skyline, and it was absolutely gorgeous. The city lights of downtown Doha provided a breathtaking distraction. There were also so many cats wandering around, and they were so adorable! For the record, cats *are* better than dogs. As much as I wanted to play with them and pet them, I opted out. After all, I'd chosen not to get a rabies vaccine before departure. As it turned out, I'd made the right decision by not playing with the cats. We quickly moved on to explore the market area and decided to meet Kaziya, who was also from the US. It was yet another maze we were trying to navigate, but eventually, we decided to meet at a Turkish restaurant. Kaziya had gone there the night before and had enjoyed it so much that she was willing to go back again. The views inside were stunning, from beautiful glass tiled walls, chandeliers, and mirrors to the detailed chairs and tables. We hoped to meet our colleagues from Japan at dinner, but as it turned out, the cats scratch! Unfortunately, my soon-to-be buddy, Jabari, had gotten scratched by a cat he'd been petting and had been rushed to the hospital to get a precautionary vaccine. Don't worry, he was OK! Since the customs line had taken so long, we didn't have a lot of time to waste in the city, so after dinner, we explored some of the markets nearby and quickly headed back toward the airport. We later got to meet the rest of the colleagues who were part of the layover at our gate, and we eagerly awaited the next leg of the trip together … to Kilimanjaro!

We landed at 7:30 a.m. after nearly thirty hours of traveling. I immediately and anxiously refreshed my AirTag location. It was still showing Miami. Ironically, the exact location it was showing in the Miami airport was a prayer room. Panic mode began. Prayers continued. I was waiting in the customs line, but the airport was small enough to see the baggage claim. I was watching bags come out when I saw a pink bag. Thank goodness. I was starting to calm down. I finally made it through customs and looked for my bag. The pink bag I had thought I'd seen wasn't in fact pink; it was a bag that had been wrapped in plastic wrap, causing it to appear pink. The bags stopped, and mine wasn't among them. They said there were no more bags. Tears were building, and I was getting emotional. I told an airport employee that my bag wasn't there. They asked for my name, and they told me they'd already known my bag wasn't there. To be fair, so had I. Airport staff confirmed Miami's early-morning message: my bag wouldn't make it. The promise of delivery the next day hung over my head. Stress and exhaustion would be accompanying me.

With tears continuing to build, I had to give the airport all my contact information and details of where I was staying, so they could deliver my bag the next day when it was expected to arrive. The whole ordeal was an unwelcome prelude to one of the most significant trips of my life. Despite my reluctance, I had little choice but to exit the airport with my colleagues and make our way to the hotel, with just my day pack on my back. After a long two-hour drive to the hotel, a pleasant surprise awaited me in the form of a welcome bag on my bed! The gift bag contained a new, clean T-shirt—an invaluable addition to my travel-worn wardrobe.

Sharing the room with Zuri eliminated the option of going entirely commando to spare myself from wearing my dirty, well-traveled clothes. We may be travel partners in crime, but we always wear clothes to sleep! *Hah!* However, the prospect of taking a shower after more than thirty hours of travel brought a wave of refreshing relief. But, considering I didn't have clean clothes other than the shirt I had just gotten, taking a shower didn't sound as satisfying. The last thing I wanted to do was clean myself and then put on dirty underwear. Consequently, I opted for a makeshift solution: handwashing my underwear in the shower and laying them to dry overnight, harboring the hope of waking up to clean underwear. I put my leggings back on for sleep. I awoke the next morning to discover that my recently washed underwear had failed to dry promptly, succumbing to the humid atmosphere and limited ventilation in the room. Undeterred, I invested approximately fifteen minutes using a hair dryer in a determined effort to expedite the drying process. The length I went to for the luxury of clean underwear was truly remarkable.

That night was a restless one as my sleep was disrupted by the relentless worry about whether my bag would arrive in time for the impending journey, causing my mind to race with anxious thoughts. Faced with limited options, I endeavored to maintain a sense of calm and divert my focus to savoring the day's activities ahead.

Our initial full day served as a crucial acclimation period, aiding us in adapting to both the elevation and the time change. Embarking on a seemingly brief thirty-minute bus ride, a concept distinctly interpreted in the unhurried pace of Tanzania, we were introduced to a world where time expanded. The rule of thumb was to always double the expected time. If someone said thirty minutes, we now knew it meant an hour. The day commenced with a captivating coffee tour, unveiling the meticulous process through which a local farmer crafts coffee entirely from scratch—an experience that unexpectedly engaged even a non-coffee-drinker like myself. Witnessing the transformation from tree beans to the aromatic elixir was a revelation, dispelling my prior ignorance. We all got to take turns crushing the beans, roasting the beans, and singing to the beans! It was fun and felt like team building among our newfound friends. Amid the anticipation for the freshly brewed coffee, we were treated to a home-cooked lunch, satisfying our appetites and providing a warm, communal respite. Although I'm not a coffee drinker, I decided to give it a taste, but I quickly regretted my decision. It was bitter and quite disgusting, if you ask me! Then again, I already knew my hatred for coffee. My new friends seemed to enjoy it. Nonetheless, I enjoyed the experience. The family also made a cute sign that said, "No Wi-Fi, talk to each other. ☺" Once our bellies were content, we eagerly embarked on the next chapter of our adventure, fueled by both culinary delight and the anticipation of the views ahead.

Anticipating the monumental task of ascending Mount Kilimanjaro, we decided to kick off our adventure with a prelude—a weeklong hike deserved an appropriate warm-up, after all. The chosen warm-up trail led us to a captivating waterfall, a natural marvel that unfolded before our eyes in all its splendor. The water's frigid temperature dissuaded me from taking a spontaneous plunge, a missed opportunity exacerbated by the absence of my suitcase. In hindsight, had it arrived, I would have discreetly sported my bathing suit beneath my clothes, ready for an invigorating dip. Some adventurous souls in our group seized the moment, braving the cold water. Although I couldn't partake, I had no regrets, given my reluctance to endure the return hike in damp attire and then endure a long, hot bus ride. Those two things combined are known to contribute to certain unwanted complications … a.k.a. yeast infections. Apologies for the candor, but it's a reality check: wet clothes and warmth can be a risky recipe for discomfort.

Our visit to the waterfall was brief as we were mindful of the impending official start of our journey the next day, emphasizing the need for a good night's sleep. Unfortunately, a good night of sleep was not in my future. The evening brought us together for dinner, fostering camaraderie and laughter as we shared stories and got to know each other better. We put all our names in a hat and randomly drew "secret buddies" to look out for throughout the trek. It was a fun start to our adventure, and would help us make sure everyone was accounted for with a group of our size. The mission was simple: always make sure that your buddy was doing well and was present among the group. But we weren't meant to reveal our buddies! It was easy to get lost in the laughter and getting to know everyone better. However, my earlier luggage ordeal persisted, and the promised arrival of my bag's arrival the next day proved to be an unfulfilled assurance, plunging me into a state of further panic.

Continuing to struggle with minimal cell service and a malfunctioning Wi-Fi connection, frustration grew with every passing moment. After what felt like an eternity, I received an update: my bag had boarded a plane from Miami to New York, continuing on to Doha, and was set to follow the trajectory of my own flight, slated to reach Tanzania at 7:30 a.m. on Wednesday. The catch? Our departure for Kilimanjaro was scheduled for just after 9:00 a.m., and the airport was in the opposite direction. Consulting with our guide, a plan emerged: depart for the airport at 6:00 a.m., aiming to intercept my bag, and then rush to join the group on the mountain.

Asha, a newfound Australian acquaintance, having met less than twenty-four hours prior, selflessly offered to accompany me, ensuring I wouldn't face the challenge alone—an act of kindness for which I remain eternally grateful. Throughout the night, I incessantly checked my AirTag for updates, tracking flights and gathering information despite the challenge of limited service. Across the globe, my significant other provided updates and even attempted to enhance my connectivity by adding additional internet service to my phone—a thoughtful gesture in the midst of my stress. Unfortunately, optimism crumbled as I learned that my bag's flight had encountered a delay, extending the landing time to 10:00 a.m. The situation became increasingly distressing, and the possibility of additional setbacks brought me to the verge of tears. I could hardly catch any shut-eye, tossing and turning, managing just about two hours of total sleep. The unfolding events kept throwing a wrench into the works, making any hope for a smooth journey seem like a distant dream.

Since the flight that had promised to have my bag had been delayed, we didn't have to leave the hotel quite as early. Around 7:00 a.m., I knocked on Asha's door and told her to get ready. We loaded up the car, and the driver efficiently transported us to the airport, reaching our destination faster than expected. With an unexpected pocket of time on our hands, my newfound companion and I strolled across the parking lot to a charming coffee and breakfast shop. There, we indulged in an unconventional yet delightful breakfast of donuts and Coca-Cola. Amid the culinary enjoyment, I couldn't escape the persistent presence of a bothersome bee, adding an amusing yet slightly exasperating element to the morning. As if my plate wasn't full enough with pretravel annoyances, here was one more buzzing around. Literally. I'm also allergic, and therefore, terrified of bees. Since conquering this journey, I've gotten stung on the ass by a bee. My fear of bees remains, and they are a literal pain in the ass.

The anticipation in the air intensified, making each passing minute feel like an eternity. Given the airport's modest size, we had the unique ability to witness planes descending in real time. I connected to the airport's Wi-Fi, constantly checking the flight status, eagerly awaiting any information on the expected landing time. The uncertainty regarding whether my bag was aboard this flight only heightened my sense of anticipation. On a side note, if you haven't experienced the convenience of the FlightAware website for tracking flights, it's a game changer. The platform allows you to trace the origins of your plane and anticipate delays based on its trajectory—a valuable tool for strategic airport planning.

Upon the plane's long-awaited touchdown, I entered the airport and made a beeline for the familiar desk where I had provided my information two days earlier. Eager to retrieve my bag, I inquired about heading to baggage claim, only to face initial denial that left me seething with frustration. Assurances of assistance from an agent proved fruitless as he disappeared into the depths of the baggage claim area, eluding my view. My patience waned as I endured the tedious wait, my attempts to catch a glimpse around the corner met with admonishment. Unperturbed, I persisted in asking when I could reclaim my bag, growing increasingly defiant. If you know me personally, you understand how much I hate being told no.

The airport's insistence that I waited until all the customers had cleared customs and collected their bags struck me as absurd. Having already endured a fifty-one-hour wait for my bag, I wasn't willing to extend my patience any further. Armed with a photo of my bag, bearing my unmistakable unique name, I sought to expedite the process. Finally, the agent emerged, seemingly ready to call it a day. Unwilling to let him slip away, I confronted him with a photo, imploring him to confirm my bag's presence. A phone call later, confirmation arrived: my bag was indeed there. Relief washed over me as I sprinted toward the long-awaited reunion. Paperwork awaited my signature before I could exit the airport, but the prospect of clean clothes was finally in my immediate future.

And so the tumultuous saga of my bag had reached its conclusion. After thirty hours of travel and fifty-one hours without my belongings, I stood on the precipice of conquering the tallest freestanding mountain in the world. The culmination of this ordeal was not just the retrieval of my possessions but also a triumphant declaration: "Let's fucking do this!"

DAY ONE:
LET'S DO THIS!

Day One: Entrance Gate to Mandara Hut | 2,700 meters (8,858 feet) | 8 kilometers (5 miles)

SLIPPING INTO FRESH, CLEAN clothes was a heightened sensation after all the travel and luggage mishaps, and possibly the best feeling in my experiences for that year thus far. With the initial flight delay threatening to shatter any hope of catching up with the group before the ascent, I was prepared for the worst. However, the Tanzanian sense of time worked in our favor. The group was tardy to the mountain, which provided us the opportunity to bridge the gap. A surge of excitement and adrenaline coursed through me, and I felt my luck slowly starting to turn around. Still, I had no idea what to expect when arriving at the gate.

As we pulled in, there was a parking lot where several other hiking groups were unloading their gear and getting ready to embark on the same adventure we soon would. Once the car was parked, I quickly unloaded my empty duffel bag and began transferring my suitcase items required for the hike into the duffel bag. The items I would need after the hike remained in my suitcase, and I put my full faith and trust in the driver that he would deliver my suitcase to the hotel for safe storage throughout the hike.

I handed my duffel bag to the porters and looked ahead to the staircase leading up to a pavilion, where we quickly identified our group! Everyone had on the same blue cotton T-shirt, so they were easily recognizable. I, however, had opted to wear a dry-fit shirt for two reasons. First, it was really hot on day one. Second, I had already worn my matching blue shirt, as it had been the only clean article of clothing I'd had during my luggage mishap. I may not have matched, but at least I knew I could easily locate my group! Among the group were porters, guides, and a local photographer we'd hired to follow us to document the journey.

Lunch was served upon arrival. The culinary offering of noodles and crisp, raw veggies doused in a vinegar sauce did little to dampen my spirits. If this was the prelude to our adventures, I was hopeful for more culinary delights ahead. Before we officially embarked on the journey, our guides and porters welcomed us with a glimpse of the vibrant energy that would be infused into the days ahead. A revelation dawned: singing and dancing would be recurrent themes throughout the trip, setting the tone for an extraordinary adventure. We joined in on the fun and eagerly embraced the journey ahead. However, a brief pause ensued as all our bags underwent meticulous scrutiny at the weighing station and security check. Nothing dangerous was coming on the mountain with us! Remember that thirty-five-pound weight limit? They did indeed check it! This process took forever, and I didn't see my duffel bag go through—which you can imagine brought back all the emotions I'd felt when my bag hadn't made it to Africa. One of the guides assured me that one of the porters had it and had already taken it through security. With that, the uncertainty dissolved, and it was time to go! By the way, a porter's job is solely to carry items up the mountain. They carry hikers' bags (up to thirty-five-pounds), along with all the cooking supplies we would need throughout the trek. I still find it hard to believe that these individuals climb a mountain carrying other people's stuff for a living. Impressive!

Inhale. Exhale. That's the mantra that echoed in my mind throughout the entire day. The hike itself, truth be told, wasn't as arduous as I had imagined. While a substantial part involved an uphill climb, it remained within the realm of achievability. I took in the rainforest views surrounding me as we began through the woods. The journey commenced at a leisurely pace, gradually building momentum as we progressed. Personally, I would have preferred a more measured pace, given the surprising challenge to catch my breath. My heart relentlessly pounded at 150 beats per minute, a steady rhythm that persisted throughout the hike. (I monitored it diligently with the help of my trusty Apple Watch, of course!)

About halfway, at four kilometers, a welcome surprise awaited: toilets! Not just any toilets, mind you, but ones equipped with the luxuries of toilet paper and running water. Despite lacking the immediate need, I compelled myself to use the facilities, unsure if such conveniences would manifest again. I might add that it was a peculiar realization to deem a hole in the ground as a luxury in the realm of toilets, but in that moment, anything seemed preferable to the alternative of squatting behind a tree. Many of my colleagues had already marked that off their lists, and I wasn't ready to join them in that feat.

The first day treated us to lush, green views as we embarked on our hike through the rainforest. At one point along the way, we also had the pleasure of seeing monkeys jumping through the trees. I was really hoping to see a toucan, but no such luck prevailed. Midway, my foot started throbbing with pain, and the strain on my shoulders from lugging my bag grew palpable. Determined to ease the burden, I resolved to lighten my day pack for the upcoming journey. My mobile pharmacy kit allowed me to mend my discomfort with an eight-hundred-milligram dose of ibuprofen. As we pressed on, the pain gradually surrendered to a numbing sensation. After an enduring four-hour trek, the sight of our camp signaled a welcome end to the day, ushering in a well-deserved evening of relaxation.

As we neared the camp, I could see a few log cabins up ahead, and the thought of relaxing and sitting down got me very excited. Before we could find our assigned cabin, we were required to check in at the main welcome cabin. We had to sign our names and enter a few other group details, but this was how they kept track of who was making their way through the different camps on the mountain. There were also signs for Wi-Fi, but it came with a price that I opted out of. My goal was to disconnect throughout this journey.

As dusk settled and we nestled into our cabin, an unexpected chill permeated the air, leaving me shivering and longing for warmth. The term "freezing" might even be an understatement. Snacking on Goldfish momentarily staved off my hunger, prompting me to embark on a quest for dinner, driven by an insatiable appetite. Amid the biting cold, I found solace in the Goldfish—a sentiment I would express time and again throughout the journey. Snack time before dinner featured popcorn, nuts, and a selection of hot beverages—tea, coffee, or hot chocolate—all of which I've never been particularly fond of. Grateful for the saving grace of Goldfish, I eagerly anticipated the heartening sustenance dinner would bring, despite my less-than-enthusiastic stance toward the drink options. Thank heavens for Goldfish, a comforting companion in the midst of the mountainous adventure.

Dinner on night one exceeded my expectations, and I actually found it genuinely delightful! A zucchini soup and bread kicked off the meal, followed by a hearty array of chicken, spaghetti noodles, potatoes, and an avocado salad. The abundance of carbs made it truly satisfying. I still am overly impressed that we had a chef join us on the trek, and their sole responsibility was to cook three meals for us each day.

Contrary to preconceived notions inspired by movies and TV, camp life didn't measure up to anticipated campfire tales and recreational activities. It was really more straightforward than that: we ate, and we slept. This realization brings to mind a valuable piece of advice imparted by our guides in the form of five golden rules to adhere to on the mountain.

1. **Stay hydrated.** Drink a lot of water.
2. **Fuel up.** Eat abundantly.
3. **Rest well.** Ensure you get ample sleep.
4. **Maintain positivity.** Stay positive at all times.
5. **Take it slow.** Walk at a leisurely pace, embracing the Swahili mantra, "Pole pole!" These guidelines became our compass, steering us through the mountainous adventure with both practicality and wisdom.

Following dinner, the guides conducted a mandatory health check, a new ritual performed twice daily to vigilantly monitor any symptoms of altitude sickness. This comprehensive examination included assessing our oxygen levels and heart rates, supplemented by a series of yes/no inquiries about potential symptoms such as headaches, appetite changes, vomiting, diarrhea, and medication intake. On the first day, my oxygen level plummeted to 94, while my pulse soared to 104. Given that my usual resting heart rate hovers around 50, this was genuinely surprising, shedding light on why I'd felt the relentless thump of my heart throughout the entire hike. The struggle intensified by my bag predicament, which had deprived me of adequate sleep the two nights prior. I'd violated rule number three before I'd even known it existed. This sleep deficit undoubtedly played a pivotal role in shaping my performance on day one.

Incidentally, the camp bathrooms continued the trend of using holes in the ground. Adding to the array of challenges, my period persisted longer than usual, possibly influenced by the altitude's impact. The inconvenience was another added struggle, but I clung to the hope that it would cease before my supplies ran out. Considering we had to use a toilet in the ground, you can only imagine the shower scenario, right? Well, here's the scoop: there were none. Surprisingly, my saving grace came in the form of body wipes which, with their refreshing minty scent, provided a semblance of cleanliness. This wasn't my ideal cleansing routine, but this journey saw me relying on unusual circumstances. Day one with no shower, and the countdown had officially begun.

Have you wondered how the hell I'm remembering all the nitty-gritty details? I get it; sometimes, I can't even remember what I had for breakfast. Early in my decision to document this journey in a book, I made a pact with myself to set aside time each evening to write before bed—a commitment to preserving the day's emotions and nuances. Despite this dedication, retaining the memories still proved challenging. If you ever embark on a similar adventure, consider keeping a journal. While photos and videos serve as memory cues, it's the act of writing down the specifics that truly etches the experience into your consciousness.

If you can imagine, after the first day of the hike, fatigue consumed me. The sleepless nights leading up to that day, fueled by the stress of my luggage debacle, had left me entirely drained. After dinner, I eagerly welcomed the prospect of rest, fully aware of the anticipated cold. Little did I expect temperatures to plummet into the forties so swiftly. Time to layer up and seek comfort in sleep!

Or so I thought. It took me forever to fall asleep, for various reasons. No matter what I tried, warmth escaped me. Sporting a beanie to shield my head from the cold, I also layered with leggings, a long-sleeve shirt, and wool socks. Even armed with a sleeping bag designed for subzero conditions, I was still assaulted by the cold. The bunk bed's thin mattress added another layer of discomfort, and because I'm a side sleeper, that posed its own challenges. Eventually, I fell into a deep sleep.

One of the compelling reasons I invited you to join me on my Kilimanjaro journey was so that I could share the genuine struggle I faced in preparing comprehensively for the trek. Certainly, I delved into books, blog posts, and videos while seeking insights. Yet what was missing were the invaluable nuggets of wisdom, like the "I wish I'd had this" or "I wish I would have done that" moments. As the cold weather of night one unfolded, I found myself longing for warmer socks and cozier pajamas, realizing my oversight in my sleep preparations. Poor planning in that department left me with only a pair of leggings and a T-shirt, a far cry from the warmth this Florida girl desperately needed. If you're embarking on a Kilimanjaro trek, let my night-one revelation guide you: pack those warm pajamas, an essential detail if you want to make it through the night in comfort. Furthermore, they make fleece liners for sleeping bags that would have been heaven-sent!

DAY TWO:
WHY IS IT WET?

Day Two: Mandara Hut to Horombo Hut | 3,720 meters (12,204 feet) | 12 kilometers (7 miles)

I WOKE UP WITH a newfound level of energy. The weight of stress from the preceding two nights had finally lifted, leaving me rejuvenated and poised for the unfolding journey of day two. Moving forward, my anxiety wouldn't hinge on the uncertainty of my belongings. However, a fresh set of concerns loomed on the horizon. Today's challenge: rain. Waking up at 5:45 a.m., after enduring a freezing and uncomfortable night, there's little worse than the realization that the sun had yet to make its appearance.

I'd opted out of packing rain pants. A gamble that, in hindsight, might not have been the wisest choice. Additionally, I hadn't opted for any fancy ponchos. Instead, my dad had handed me two of those one-dollar plastic, piece-of-shit ponchos before my departure. Spoiler alert: they worked. To some extent, at least. Maybe they aren't so shitty after all.

After waking up and getting dressed for the day, the next order of business was packing up—all part of the routine to facilitate our porters' parallel journey. My choice of a vibrant teal duffel bag proved strategic, effortlessly distinguishing it from the sea of other bags and ensuring my porter always located it promptly. With our essentials packed, we descended downstairs to the dining area for an early breakfast, which was an unusual 6:30 a.m. affair for me, but I knew I needed fuel.

The initial offering was a peculiar porridge with a soupy consistency and unwelcome chunks—a less-than-appetizing start. Determined to fuel up, I improvised by adding peanut butter to salvage the flavor, but it only worked to a modest degree. A piece of papaya followed, disappointingly reminiscent of dirt. Relief came with the arrival of bread, paired with eggs. Applying a generous slather of fake butter to the bread and drowning the eggs in ketchup became my culinary survival strategy. My favorite part was the conclusion of breakfast. We were pleasantly surprised with mango juice and bananas! Let me tell you, that burst of sugar proved to be my much-needed saving grace! Another looking-back moment: since I didn't care for the hot beverage options, I would have loved to have packed juice boxes to have with breakfast. Add that your list!

Following our newfound morning routine, it was time for our morning health checks! My oxygen level had held steady at 93, and my heart rate was 59, showing significant improvement from the previous night—a clear indication of the restorative power of a good night's sleep. Despite lingering fatigue, I felt surprisingly decent. By 7:45 a.m., we were geared up and on our way, greeted by a frigid forty-nine-degree temperature, a striking challenge for this Floridian. Adding to the already brisk conditions, rain accompanied us. I bundled up, trying to prepare for the elements that lay ahead.

Throughout the entire day, a persistent question echoed in my mind: "Will we ever be dry?" Unfortunately, the resounding answer seemed to be a strong no. The terrain began to steepen after the third hour of climbing. Surprisingly, the foot pain that had plagued me on day one was entirely absent, transforming the hike into a markedly different experience. With improved energy, a new mindset, and a commendable pace, I found myself navigating the challenging ascent with newfound ease. The views however, were very anticlimactic given the dense fog accompanied by the rain. I had been looking forward to taking in the views, but I chose to remember rule number four and maintain a positive mindset.

Around the fourth hour, a welcome sight appeared: picnic tables sheltered by a pavilion that mercifully shielded us from the relentless rain. And, to my delight, more drop toilets awaited! Who knew that I would find joy in toilets? Certainly not I! There was one unfortunate downside: their distinct and unpleasant odor. These were the worst-smelling toilets so far. Despite the discomfort, I refrained from making excessive complaints, acknowledging the luxury of privacy and the avoidance of the squat-in-the-woods scenario during a downpour. I laughed at myself, determined to keep that particular skill off my résumé. Meanwhile, my colleagues, unphased by such considerations, continued their frequent pee breaks every thirty minutes. Yes, behind any bush available (for now). After our bathroom break was finished, we spent a solid ten to fifteen minutes resting, eating little snacks, and ensuring we remained hydrated. Unfortunately, there were no sitting breaks since everything was soaked.

The rain showed no mercy, persisting throughout the entire five-hour hike that concluded around 1:00 p.m. As we wrapped up, the rain persisted, and the temperature dropped again, to forty-four degrees. After braving a lengthy hike in the cold rain, the highlight of our day emerged with the much-anticipated hot lunch. A collective team cheer erupted as noodles, potatoes, chicken stew, veggies, and pineapple graced our plates. The food tasted heavenly, although the freezing and wet conditions likely enhanced its appeal. Grateful for the waterproof factor of my boots, I believed they had done a commendable job of preserving the dryness of my feet—until, of course, reality set it. The toll of a five-hour walk had diminished my energy. After lunch, exhaustion enveloped me, and seizing the opportunity, I indulged in a quick nap. As it turned out, mountain naps swiftly secured a spot as my newfound favorite indulgence.

Amid my nap, a sudden thought disrupted my peace: "What is that dripping sound? Seriously, haven't we had our fair share of moisture today?" To my dismay, water was dripping onto my bunk bed (I happened to be on the bottom bunk). The source of the water was promptly identified; it was my bunk mate's open and leaking CamelBak. Fortunately, we acted quickly to address the situation. Despite the minor hiccup, nap time proved successful, except for the persistent chill that had settled into my toes. In our cabin, a collective state of cold, wet discomfort prevailed, reaching a point where distinguishing between what was cold and what was wet became a challenging endeavor. My initially trustworthy boots, which I'd believed earlier had kept my feet dry, now felt alarmingly drenched. All I could think was, "I hope they're dry come morning!" A valuable note to self: perhaps bringing something to absorb moisture would have been a wise move. Well, there's always next time. (Psych!)

Post nap activities transitioned seamlessly into snack time, transforming into an impromptu bonding session for the group. At this camp, we were divided into smaller cabins, and thus, we were separated from the dining room. After a quick walk across the camp, the fun began. Engaged in games, half of us reveled in a round of Uno while the other half immersed themselves in a lively Heads Up! competition. Patiently waiting out the time until dinner, it was fulfilling to witness everyone enjoying themselves. Despite enduring a collectively miserable day in the rain, the camaraderie remained undampened, and spirits were surprisingly high. Not a hint of altitude sickness had surfaced among us, and the shared enthusiasm for the ongoing adventure was quite noticeable.

Dinner continued to be a source of joy, and the flavors were absolutely delightful. I was consistently impressed by the culinary prowess of our chef, who managed to prepare such delicious meals on the mountain. You might be curious about how they managed to feed us up there. Well, some of the porters took on the responsibility of carrying the food supplies. Similar to how they handled our bags, these dedicated porters lugged the ingredients to our camp each day, ensuring we had sustenance. I still find it remarkable that this was part of their job. The porters were truly incredible, and our journey would have been far more challenging without their invaluable support. For this meal, they treated us to a decadent butternut soup accompanied by bread, while the main course featured rice, beef in an intriguing sauce, and a medley of veggies. And, to our delight, we were also served refreshing orange slices. Hooray for a touch of sugar! If you've caught on to the routine, you'll know it was time for yet another round of heath checks. By the end of day two, my stats were still looking great with an oxygen level of 92 and a heart rate at 86 beats per minute. I was beginning to feel very proud of my lungs for keeping up with the climbing elevation (no pun intended).

I ventured back to the cabin, preparing myself for another chilly night's rest. Surprisingly, it was only 8:34 p.m., yet my entire cabin had already succumbed to the embrace of sleep. Taking this as my cue, I decided to join them. After all, scribbling in my journal with a headlamp on in the dark probably would have made for a comical sight. However, another valuable lesson from my mountain experience was that I never once cared about my appearance. Mirrors were hardly a concern, makeup was abandoned, and the liberating feeling of not being preoccupied with how I looked was truly refreshing.

DAY THREE:
ACCLIMATION DAY

Day Three: Acclimation Day: Horombo Hut to Zebra Rock and Back to Horombo Hut | 4,315 meters (14,156 feet) | 10 kilometers (6 miles)

DURING THE PREVIOUS NIGHT, the struggle to find warmth seemed eternal as I battled the biting cold, particularly in my feet. Seeking solace, I resorted to placing hand warmers at the bottom of my sleeping bag and in my socks, and once I finally drifted into sleep, the night unfolded in tranquility. Anticipating the frigid temperatures, I strategically nestled all of my clothes intended for the day in the warm cocoon of my sleeping bag. Though navigating a night in forty-degree weather wasn't exactly a joy, I harbored gratitude for the shelter we had, realizing that camping in tents outdoors would have presented a far more daunting challenge. Some hikers opt to take one of the other five paths up the mountain, which does require outdoor camping. No, thank you!

A peculiar difficulty presented itself when my trusty Vaseline, the tube designed for lip care, submitted to the freezing temperatures, rendering it unusable. However, a simple remedy unfolded as I stowed it in my pocket overnight, and I'm delighted to report that it was revived. Curious about my nighttime attire? Picture this: ski socks, leggings, a sports bra, a long-sleeve thermal layer, a cozy fleece pullover, and my reliable summit jacket. They say wearing less layers keeps you warm in a sleeping bag, but I beg to differ. That method did not work for me. Instead, I chose the Eskimo life. A whisper of concern lingered as I contemplated whether these layers would suffice for the impending summit night if they hardly kept me warm while sleeping.

We found ourselves awake at the early hour of 6:30 a.m., even though our official wake-up time wasn't until 7:00, or better yet, 7:30 a.m. The scheduled delivery of warm water for washing was set for 7:00, a luxury I decided to forgo. Bathing with body wipes posthike had proven effective, and I was unwilling to expend additional energy on a warm-water cleanse in the freezing outdoors. No, thank you.

Despite the supposed breakfast time of 7:40 a.m. on day three, my experiences in Africa had taught me that time held little significance. A porter arrived with hot water, and we seized the opportunity to request the drying of our boots, which were still soaked from the previous day's relentless rain. Although my boots hadn't felt wet during the hike, the moisture in the air had made it challenging to discern their true condition. The silver lining was that day three would entail only a brief hike. We were acclimating, ascending to a point known as Zebra Rock, and then descending back to the same camp for sleep. This strategic acclimation period was aimed at making day four more manageable as we would be continuing our ascent and gaining even more elevation.

As the morning sun graced our camp, breakfast unfolded with an unexpected addition: hot dogs, accompanied by a medley of bread, pancakes, and more eggs. It was at this juncture that my aversion to rubbery eggs emerged, and I gracefully chose to opt out. Surprisingly, the hot dog proved to be a delightful alternative, offering sustenance for the journey ahead. Another strange revelation was that I enjoyed eating hot dogs for breakfast. Who would have thought? The entire group continued to bask in good health, free from the clutches of altitude sickness, and I fervently wished for this positive state to endure through the remainder of our ascent. After all, day three marked the official midpoint of our expedition!

Embarking on our trek to Zebra Rock around 9:45 a.m., we captured captivating photos along the way, blessed with the presence of the sun, a welcome relief after the previous day's rain. The hike unfolded with relative ease, though a subtle headache attempted to make its presence known. Quickly dispelling the discomfort, I reminded myself that sugar often works wonders in such situations. Our ascent reached an elevation of approximately 4,100 meters before descending back to the camp. Unfortunately, the apex of today's climb greeted us with dense clouds, obscuring what we imagined to be breathtaking views. The view of Zebra Rock, however, was fascinating. Imagine a rock with white and black markings that truly resemble the markings on a zebra. We stopped to take a group photo here, and it became one of my favorite views. Undeterred by the dense fog, we navigated the three-hour stroll, descending to the dining area for a well-deserved lunch upon our return.

Lunch began with the guides presenting a piping hot soup, albeit a tad too generous with the pepper for my spice-sensitive palate. (I'll say it: I'm a wimp.) The main course was a medley of bread paired with peanut sauce, assorted veggies bathed in a savory sauce, potatoes, beans, and a refreshing assortment of oranges and watermelon. The eclectic variety was both surprising and peculiar in its combination, creating a unique feast for our mountain-bound appetites. On another note, the revelation that we had passed the last primary water source on the mountain hinted at the forthcoming change in amenities: flushing toilets would no longer grace our camp, marking a transition to an even more rustic mountain experience.

As the day progressed, it was time for another glorious nap. Scratch that. It was time for another freezing nap. In hindsight, a fleece blanket would have been a welcome addition inside my sleeping bag, offering both warmth and versatility for chilly excursions to the dinner table. My wish list grew to include fleece-lined camp shoes and a lightweight pair of gloves—essential gear I hadn't anticipated. While the movement from hiking had shielded me from the biting cold, the stillness at camp proved challenging. As a Sunshine State resident accustomed to warmth, the cold's grip on me was unwelcome. Remember the rain from yesterday? The wetness still clung to our clothes, compelling us to fashion a makeshift clothesline using hiking poles that ingeniously extended from the window to the bunk bed's edge. Against all odds, the impromptu solution proved effective. Another lesson learned on the mountain that day: we saw a Land Rover! This sparked curiosity as to how vehicles could navigate the rugged terrain. Later, we discovered its role in transporting supplies and serving as a rescue vehicle when necessary—a testament to the mountain's dynamic infrastructure. Further along in the journey, that vehicle would play another role.

The time struck 5:30 p.m., which marked the time to gather in the dining area for snacks. Anticipating the usual fare of bland popcorn, I wisely opted to bring a bag of Goldfish, offering a savory and satisfying snack. While we were awaiting dinner, the moment had finally arrived to immerse ourselves in the captivating melodies the guides had been serenading us with throughout the expedition. Our guide transcribed the lyrics onto paper, and we dedicated ourselves to rehearsing the songs repeatedly until the harmonies became ingrained into our experience. Finally, the ambiance of my camp expectations were coming to fruition. We may not have sat around a campfire listening to someone play guitar while singing along, but this certainly sufficed!

I grabbed a picture of the lyrics so I could practice. Here's what we worked off of.

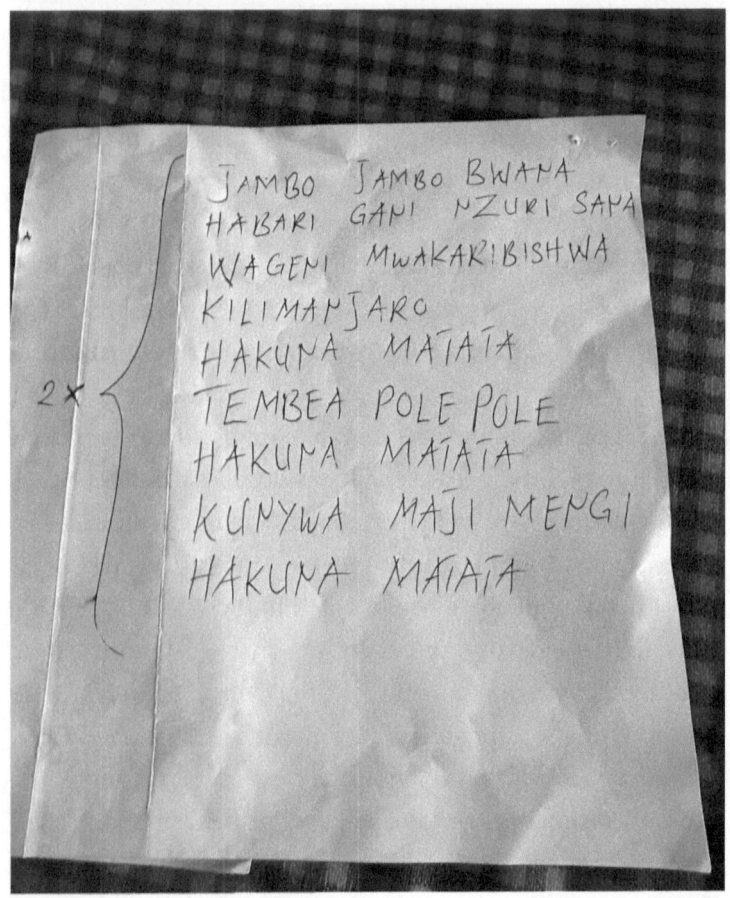

"Jambo Bwana" song lyrics.

You're going to have to google that one if you want to know the full meaning. But I do know that "hakuna matata" means "no worries" (for the rest of our days)—thanks to the classic childhood movie, *The Lion King.* "Pole pole" means "to walk slowly." The rest is something about foreigners being welcome, and that you'll get there safe, no worries. Either way, it's a catchy song and was frequently sang after that day.

Dinner that evening failed to leave a lasting impression, as my recollection of the served meal is hazy, devoid of both details from my journal and photos to jog my memory. What I can affirm, however, is that there was a discernible waning of my appetite, signaling potential challenges for the upcoming two days with a notable lack of culinary enthusiasm. I will put it plainly: I had no desire to eat. Given the rigorous daily hikes, I easily surpassed burning three thousand calories daily, and it was imperative that I consume calories, so I wasn't sure how I'd keep going without a desire to eat. I'll spare you the repetition of the previous day's routines, but rest assured, the cold weather persisted as bedtime approached.

DAY FOUR: DESERT SMURF

Day Four: Horombo Hut to Kibo Hut | 4,703 meters (15,429 feet) | 10 kilometers (6 miles)

AS THE DAYS GREW longer, the desire to remember the details escaped me. I started journaling less and less, and I started living more in the moment. As I write this book, I am annoyed that I neglected to write a lot about the details in the later days. What I may have failed to mention is that I spent some time each day capturing footage on my GoPro. I used the clamp attachment to secure it to the strap on my day pack. I always started and ended each hike with a video so I could time-stamp our departures and arrivals. Throughout each day, I'd film sporadically depending on the scenery. This really helped me remember the details of the scenery. In hindsight, I could have done the same from my phone, but I liked the hands-free option of the GoPro and having all my videos and pictures in one designated place. While the details were slowly fading, one thing did cross my mind on that day: "How the hell is it Friday?" Despite all the challenges I'd endured to that point, time seemed to be passing quickly. We ate breakfast around 7:00 a.m. and were served more hot dogs, oranges, cucumbers, eggs, and toast with jelly. I pushed my eggs aside and nibbled on everything else. My egg aversion was in full swing. At least I was able to eat everything else without too much disgust.

Day four would bring us to base camp and a trek through the desert, with our journey commencing early, around 8:00 a.m. I couldn't believe how many different vegetation zones there were on Kilimanjaro. Each day brought new views, and I always looked forward to the scenery. What does a desert on Kilimanjaro look like, you might wonder? Exactly how you would think! There were endless stretches of sand with minimal vegetation. The barrenness presented a challenge for my fellow hikers who were seeking discreet spots for nature's call, given the scarcity of bushes. My commitment to using only the drop toilets behind closed doors persisted. It's worth noting, as I've failed to mention this, that you must bring your own toilet paper or wipes unless you fancy the alternative of air-drying. These are a must-have to keep in your day pack! Of course, there's always the option to stand while peeing! Anticipating the need to navigate the wild for bathroom breaks, I brought a GoGirl device, although fortunately, I didn't find it necessary, thanks to the drop toilets. If you're not sure what that is, it's a small silicone device for women that allows you to urinate while standing.

The day's hiking gear differed slightly from the days prior and included a sun hat and layers in the morning as the day began with crisp air. In an effort to stay warm and shield my face from the swirling desert sand, I opted for a neck gaiter, a decision that would unknowingly provide comedic relief later. As the morning progressed and temperatures climbed, I decided to remove the gaiter during our first break. To my surprise, Zuri inquired, "Danica, why are you blue?" Perplexed, I looked down at my outfit, which was a display of blue and purple, assuming that was what she had been referencing. I responded, "What's wrong with my outfit? You know I like to match!" This was part of the reason I hadn't wanted to rent my gear if my luggage had not made it. Matching was important to me! Zuri then explained to me that my face and lips had taken on a blue hue. Mild panic set in as I wondered if I was unknowingly cold or if the elevation had triggered some peculiar skin discoloration. Although I had been committed to not caring about my appearance, and the lack of mirrors, I resorted to using my phone's camera to check out my face. It turned out that the culprit had been my unwashed neck gaiter. Note to self: wash new items before wearing them. Having unexpectedly transformed into a Smurf for the day, I embraced it.

The concern of resembling a Smurf quickly faded into insignificance as a smaller challenge on that eventful day. Throughout the entire trek, my appearance had been a minimal concern, and I genuinely mean that! However, the weight of my day pack intensified with each step, causing me to lean forward to alleviate the mounting pressure on my back. Being the stubborn woman that I am, I chose to endure the pain in silence. Yet my persistent lifting of the backpack did not escape the notice of my fellow trekkers, prompting inquiries about my well-being. Attempting to downplay the situation, I assured them that I would be fine, and that my back was only bothering me slightly. However, their concern prevailed, and they managed to convince me to let one of the guides shoulder the burden of my backpack. It was a challenging moment for me, grappling with the conflicting emotions of perceived defeat and reluctance to accept help. My stubborn independence, coupled with a reluctance to reveal vulnerability, made it difficult for me to relinquish control. The guide offered a piece of wisdom that resonated: "No one is going to ask if you carried your backpack the entire hike. They will be more interested in hearing if you made it to the top!" In hindsight, he had been right. Now you know my secret! The decision to let go of my bag on day four became a pivotal moment, and the success of the rest of the trek hinged on that choice. It can be hard to put your pride aside, but ultimately, who cares what other people think? I've never been one to care too much about others' opinions of me, and this trip didn't change that.

The day proved to be both lengthy and challenging due to steepness, yet it unfolded against a backdrop of breathtaking views. The desert trek offered us the exhilarating sight of Kilimanjaro's majestic peak on the horizon, injecting a renewed sense of excitement and anticipation into our journey. Amid the awe-inspiring scenery, an unexpected surprise awaited us: a group of mountain bikers! Yes, you read that correctly. To my disbelief, a cohort of mountain bikers effortlessly passed us on the trail. While logistics of their ascent to the summit remained a mystery, I speculated that they might have biked to the base camp, requiring a subsequent hike to reach the summit. Regardless of their route, I couldn't help but marvel at their remarkable feat of biking on Kilimanjaro. Capturing the moment on video and in photographs, I ensured that this unique encounter would be etched in my memory.

Mountain biker on Kilimanjaro.

We embraced the "slow and steady wins the race" mantra throughout this six-mile hike, lasting just over six hours. If you're good at math, you will figure that we had a pace of one mile per hour. We truly walked so slowly. Climbing Kilimanjaro is no quick feat. You must take one small step after another. I've since told many friends that training for Kilimanjaro doesn't have to be about how many miles you can complete, but rather, how long you can slowly walk. Upon arriving at base camp, our anticipation was heightened, but we had to wait until the cabins were ready. In the interim, we seized the opportunity to capture some picturesque moments. My favorite thing about being at base camp was the feeling of being in the clouds! As a young girl, I'd always thought it possible to jump from cloud to cloud. Seeing the clouds from that high up was a sight I will never forget. Once I got my cloud fix, it was time to embark on an exploration of the camp's facilities.

To my dismay, the bathroom area left a lasting unwelcome impression. Stepping outside, a pungent odor permeated the air, intensified by a light, misty rain and shrouded sun. It marked the first time I had to resort to plugging my nose while relieving myself, desperate to ward off the nauseating stench. As raindrops continued their gentle descent, I silently prayed for a reprieve before our impending summit attempt. Glancing at my Apple Watch, which miraculously retained functionality despite the lack of cell service, I noticed a chilling forty-seven-degree temperature, with a hopeful forecast of rain ceasing around 7:00 p.m. Skeptical of the accuracy without reliable connectivity, I reflected on the limited texting ability I had enjoyed during the initial three days. The limited texting meant that I was able to send a quick text to my family to update them on my progress, and that I would soon lose service. The service was not reliable, and it took several minutes to send one message. So, if you're planning on texting while on the mountain … don't. Although there was the ability to access paid Wi-Fi at the camps, I provide you a friendly reminder that I chose to remain blissfully disconnected from social media and interactions with others.

The remaining activities for the day at base camp followed a familiar pattern: lunch, nap time, dinner, and eventually, sleep. However, I came to consider it more of an extended nap, as you'll soon discover. Despite ongoing struggles with my appetite, lunch brought a delightful surprise: chicken wings and potato wedges, a taste of home! The abundance of potatoes was particularly satisfying. Our lunch concluded around 3:00, and we had a brief window to nap before dinner at 5:30.

The characteristic African approach to time persisted, and as expected, dinner faced a delay. However, the silver lining was that dinner was served in our building this time, a welcome convenience given the persistent rainy weather outside. The evening meal comprised soup, noodles, and somewhat unappetizing cooked veggies. My appetite remained modest, and I found solace in my trusty Goldfish snacks. Following dinner, the debrief extended longer than desired, and we were growing weary. The final health checks revealed an oxygen level of 88 and a heart rate of 90. Surprisingly, I was relieved that my oxygen level hadn't dipped lower.

We were finally dismissed to bed where we could catch two hours of sleep if we played our cards right. We had to be back in the dining area by 11:00 p.m. to prep for the highly anticipated summit night.

SUMMIT NIGHT: ZOMBIE APOCALYPSE

Day Five: Kibo Hut to Uhuru Peak | 5,895 meters (19,340 feet) | 6 kilometers (4 miles)
Uhuru Peak to Kibo Hut | 6 kilometers (4 miles)

THE TIME WAS 11:19 P.M. The cabin was quiet but active as fellow trekkers layered up in anticipation of the upcoming summit. Despite the chilly exterior, the ambient temperature was bearable, a stark contrast to the nauseating odors emanating from the bathrooms. Seizing a moment before donning my final layers, I ventured to the restroom, only to be greeted by a horrible stench. The deplorable condition revealed a disheartening sight: someone had missed the drop toilet entirely, literally shitting on the floor. The experience was nothing short of appalling, and I couldn't begin to fathom subjecting myself to such shame. It was the most unpleasant bathroom experience of my entire life.

As I readied myself for the summit, the prospect of immersing myself in music to pass the time was appealing. Alas, my playlist was limited to "Haven't Met You Yet" by Michael Bublé and "Dicked Down in Dallas" by Trey Lewis, neither of which seemed fitting for the momentous occasion. The thought of those two tracks on a loop throughout the night didn't quite resonate with the gravity of the climb. Thankfully, amid my limited musical choices, I stumbled upon a lone podcast, "Real AF" by Andy Frisella, previously downloaded on my phone. No, this isn't an endorsement; it's merely a recommendation to explore his motivational content. With no alternative at hand, I embraced the podcast episodes as my companions on this "solitary" journey.

We congregated in the dining area, seeking warmth from the customary array of hot beverage choices: hot water, instant coffee, hot chocolate, or tea. Accompanying this, we were treated to cookies reminiscent of the Biscoff variety found on Delta Air Lines. As we refilled our water bottles, the anticipation of the impending briefing grew. With the ascent, the temperature was set to plummet, and the real concern was our water bottles freezing. The remedy? Keep them upside down. For those utilizing hydration packs, a nifty trick was shared: blowing warm air back through the tube to eliminate freezing.

We were at last poised to embark on our eagerly anticipated summit night! The culmination of nine months of anticipation was finally unfolding before us. However, the most formidable challenge I faced was my overwhelming fatigue.

I had anticipated an adrenaline surge upon waking up, envisioning it as the force that would propel me through the night. Regrettably, that burst of energy failed to materialize.

Despite the initial cold, I had layered up with ski pants, thermal leggings, hiking socks, wool socks, ski gloves, a neck gaiter, ear warmers, a beanie, a long-sleeve thermal, a long-sleeve dry-fit, a fleece jacket, and my summit jacket—transforming into an Eskimo-like figure. A headlamp illuminated my path through the pitch-black darkness outside. The trek commenced at a pace slower than any we had maintained during the entire hike. While the deliberate speed was justified by the challenging incline and elevation, it introduced the added challenge of staying warm.

As we ascended, the mantra "One foot in front of the other" echoed in my mind, a rallying cry to combat the fatigue that had taken on a new depth of meaning. Guides tapping me on the back became a regular occurrence, urging me to stay awake and keep moving. The advice included stomping my feet on the ground if I felt tired. Despite my attempts, it seemed ineffective. I longed for a power nap, but the cold and exhaustion intensified.

Approximately two hours into the climb, as we reached our first stopping point, the biting cold left me unable to feel my feet. During the break, I resorted to placing hand warmers in my boots and gloves to revive sensation. Seated on a rock, I attempted a brief respite by lying down, only to be promptly interrupted by the guides instructing me to open my eyes. Frustration welled up; all I sought was a fleeting five-minute power nap to reclaim a semblance of vitality. I was so annoyed in that moment. The prospect of continuing the ascent seemed increasingly daunting.

As one of the guides kindly carried my day pack on summit night, his presence remained a comforting assurance, allowing me to take occasional sips of water as we ascended. Regrettably, my lapse in attention caused my water to freeze, imposing an unintended hydration hiatus until our descent commenced. However, the camaraderie among my fellow trekkers shone through, as they graciously shared their water supply during the challenging climb. In addition to this, I found solace in snacking on my trusty Goldfish, a reliable source of sustenance that provided both energy and a momentary relief.

Upon enduring a grueling five-hour climb, our collective efforts culminated at the first peak, Gilman's Point, standing proudly at an elevation of 5,685 meters (18,652 feet). Approximately thirty minutes after reaching this pinnacle, the gradual ascent of the sun bathed the surroundings in a warm glow, infusing the atmosphere with a newfound vigor. The unfolding panorama from this elevated vantage point was nothing short of awe-inspiring, the breathtaking scenery enhanced by the mesmerizing trail of headlamps dotting the path below. As the first rays of light pierced through the clouds, the distant city lights began to twinkle, creating a surreal and enchanting spectacle.

By 6:00 a.m., our determined ascent led us to the next pinnacle, Stella Point, perched at an elevation of 5,756 meters (18,885 feet). Despite the burgeoning daylight, the prevailing wind intensified at this juncture, challenging our resolve. A brief surprise awaited us here, where we savored revitalizing sips of orange juice. The diminishing distance to the ultimate summit became palpable, heightening our anticipation. The breathtaking sunrise we experienced at Stella Point was the inspiration behind the cover of *Kilimanjaro Unfiltered*. I don't know if I will ever capture a more beautiful sunrise photo. This one is literally "for the books"! The journey unfolded into captivating sights of craters and glaciers, accompanied by a fleeting snowfall that, albeit picturesque, added a layer of complexity as the swirling snow and gusty winds briefly metamorphosed the landscape into a temporary blizzard, rendering visibility a formidable challenge.

While I continued to focus on the words of my podcast in an effort to remain awake, I realized that I was in my own little world. I genuinely had little to no idea how other people were holding up, because I was largely focused on my own survival. I think at least three people did finally experience altitude sickness during summit night. I saw one girl go slightly off-trail to puke, and I heard stories of others who were puking every few minutes. I'm so grateful the Diamox medication had done its job and prevented any altitude sickness.

At approximately 7:28 a.m. on October 7, 2023, the triumphant moment arrived as we reached the summit of Kilimanjaro. I did it! Witnessing the sign was the culmination of all my efforts. Uhuru Peak, standing tall at 5,895 meters

(19,340 feet) marked the climax of achievement—Africa's highest point and the world's tallest freestanding mountain. Notably, it is also one of the globe's largest inactive volcanoes. Despite the recent snowfall obscuring the summit sign, I found a unique charm in its weathered appearance. How was the weather at the top? *Cold.* Freezing. Below freezing. But adrenaline can certainly make you not pay attention to that. After seeing the sign, I finally felt awake again.

The one disappointment that lingered in my mind was not insisting on capturing an individual photo with the summit sign. After enduring a grueling seven-hour ascent, and battling freezing temperatures and overwhelming fatigue, the opportunity for a personal snapshot was overshadowed by the constraint of time and the presence of another sizable group sharing the summit moment. The guides, mindful of the potential risks of altitude sickness, limited our stay at the peak to a mere five to ten minutes. While I managed to squeeze in a group photo and a hurried selfie, the desire for a more personal memento persisted. Nonetheless, the collective image and spontaneous selfie serve as tangible reminders of an unforgettable achievement, etching the memory forever in my mind.

Hence, the trials and tribulations of the past five days took on a newfound significance, rendering the obstacles and challenges faced during the ascent inconsequential. The ultimate objective had been achieved: all twenty of us had successfully reached the summit of Kilimanjaro. Yet the journey wouldn't conclude at the peak; it mandated retracing our steps back to the starting point.

Group photo at the top of Mount Kilimanjaro.

Selfie with Mount Kilimanjaro Uhuru Peak sign.

You may wonder why we began the summit in the middle of the night, and I still ask myself this question. I think there were a number of reasons, including the foot traffic on the mountain, not being able to see what was ahead of us (yes, that's a good thing), and ultimately, leading to the most epic views of the sunrise. Although I was uncomfortably cold and faced extreme sleep deprivation, the illuminating lights from all the hikers' headlamps was also a unique view I will likely never experience again.

While the ascent to the summit demanded approximately seven and a half hours, the descent back to base camp was accomplished in a mere three and a half hours—almost half the time. Throughout the ascent, we'd navigated a series of switchbacks due to the steep terrain and had even confronted formidable boulders along the way. Finally, all the box jumps at CrossFit proved valuable! Despite being informed that we would retrace our path on the descent, this turned out to be untrue. Instead, the majority of the descent involved a challenging decline akin to skiing through gravel rocks. Believe it or not, the hiking poles, which had been a constant companion, finally proved their worth during this downward journey. I found myself sliding through the rocks with a sensation reminiscent of skiing down mountains in Colorado, albeit sans snow and with a noticeable dustiness in the air. Unfortunately, on the way down, one of our colleagues tweaked her knee and got hurt pretty badly. But, at that elevation, there were limited options to get down, so she had to power through.

Descending offered equally breathtaking views, and I progressed as swiftly as my endurance allowed, fueled by the anticipation of much-needed sleep. One standout moment on the journey down to base camp occurred when the group stopped to sit and take in the views. We probably spent about ten to twenty minutes taking in the views together. This became another one of my favorite photographed moments.

Enjoying the view.

Upon reaching base camp, regrettably, sleep would be delayed for several more hours. A brief nap was all we could afford before undertaking the next leg of our journey to the subsequent camp, entailing another grueling four-hour expedition.

Before entering the cabin, the porters took the time to brush off the accumulated dust from our ski pants, a consequence of navigating through rocky terrain. Despite the fatigue looming over us, there was one more delightful hurdle to overcome before settling in for a much-needed nap: lunch! Despite my somewhat diminished appetite, the prospect of a hearty meal elicited genuine excitement. The meal turned out to be an unexpected delight as we were treated to a steaming bowl of ramen with chicken broth, accompanied by noodles and toast. It was a surprising and satisfying culinary respite, turning what might have been a simple meal into a cherished experience at high altitude.

As I embraced the opportunity for a brief nap, I decided to capture the moment with a selfie. My eyes reflected the glossiness brought on by sleep deprivation, while my face, nose, and lips displayed the toll of the harsh summit night: swollen and weather-beaten by the extreme cold. While acknowledging it as perhaps one of my least flattering selfies, it simultaneously stands as a testament to my strength and resilience, symbolizing the myriad challenges conquered on my journey to the summit of Kilimanjaro. Grateful for the unfiltered authenticity, I cherish this snapshot as a poignant reminder of the arduous but triumphant ascent.

Selfie after summiting Mount Kilimanjaro.

DAYS FIVE TO SIX: THE DESCENT

Days Five to Six: Kibo Hut to Horombo Hut | 2,700 meters (8,858 feet) | 10 kilometers (6 miles)
Horombo Hut to Marangu Gate | 20 kilometers (12 miles)

DAYS FIVE AND SIX morphed into one really long day, or so it felt. It was hard to keep track of what day it was at this point. After the nap at Kibo Hut (base camp), we packed our duffel bags and handed them off to the porters one final time for the start of our descent. Our journey would first involve walking back through the desert and taking a six-mile journey back to Horombo Hut, where we'd spent day two of the hike. This part of the journey is still a blur to me. It took us about four hours to make it down to the camp, and once the cabins were visible from the trail, a small victory emerged. I couldn't wait for a full night of sleep.

Remember the girl who had hurt her knee on the mountain descent? Well, I don't remember all of the specific details, but what I can tell you is that she got transported to a certain marker on the mountain and was helicoptered to the hospital for inspection. Spoiler alert: she was OK, but she had to get a knee brace and crutches for the rest of the trip. The important thing was that she was OK. I share these details not to scare you, but to outline the reality and possibility of getting injured during the trek. The only other injury I was aware of was a minor toe injury where another girl had decided to take advantage of that rescue Land Rover we had seen earlier in the trip. She hitched a ride to the bottom, skipping the final day of walking. I was envious, but at the same time, I was willing to keep enduring pain to satisfy my mission of summiting *and* descending Kilimanjaro.

I'll tell you what I remember from the final day. We started fairly early with the goal of returning to the entrance by early afternoon. I decided to start at the front of the group for the descent. The only things on my mind were getting back to the bottom, getting my hands on a cold beverage, and waiting for the long-anticipated shower. But, of course, there would be a few final challenges to face. However, this time, there was some comedic relief. The group I'd decided to walk with ended up being a group I felt like I was running with. Their pace was insanely fast, and at times, I found myself jogging to keep up with them. My "secret buddy" Jabari was part of this fast group, though, so I finally got to see how he was doing with the trek. We hadn't gotten to spend much time together since he was such a quick walker! Eventually, we got separated, and I was alone in the middle of Kilimanjaro. While it was peaceful, part of me was also scared of being alone out there. If something happened, no one would know. Coincidentally, something did happen. I mentioned earlier that, throughout my journey, I had done my best to get GoPro footage daily so I could remember the views and create a video. I hadn't been able to use it on summit night, however, due to the extreme cold and not wanting to deal with it. Instead, I'd occasionally used my phone to capture pictures and some quick videos. I also hadn't used the GoPro when heading down since I had already seen the terrain on the way up. But, as I strolled along the trail solo, I decided to make a quick video on my phone to talk about being alone on the mountain. I panned around to take in the views, and as soon as I went to film behind me, I tripped on a rock and came crashing down, phone and all. I immediately got back up, dusted off my dirty hands, and said, "Well, this is going to make for a great video!" And I can assure you that it did, indeed. My phone quickly went back in my bag after that. When in doubt, something fun or unexpected always seems to happen. I ended up being alone for about thirty minutes when I was finally able to catch up to the group.

As we began the final two hours, I could feel blisters forming on my right foot. For sure, I thought I had escaped blisters; but leave it to the last day to ruin that streak. The downhill motion and the speed at which we were descending played a role in the blisters forming. The constant friction of my foot rubbing with each downhill step was unwelcome. I had no choice but to deal with the discomfort and await the outcome. The farther we walked, the more impatient I grew with reaching the entrance—it felt like forever away. At every turn, I kept hoping to see civilization, an opening, some indication that we were close. Finally, after the fourth hour, we finally reached the gate! It felt so victorious to be done! I couldn't wait to sit down and relax, but the thing I wanted the most was Coca-Cola. I craved sugar and a cold beverage more than I ever had in my life. To my surprise, the gift shop at the gate sold them for one dollar. It was a very happy moment to get my hands on an ice-cold Coke. Before we could do that, however, we had to sign the guest book to formalize our exit. Just before noon on October 8, 2023, I exited the Marangu Route of Mount Kilimanjaro. The mission was officially accomplished.

It's still hard to believe that we'd spent nearly five days hiking to the summit of Kilimanjaro, and in a matter of one day, we'd reached the bottom. The path up is the same path down, and it ends up being about a fifty-mile journey.

As I sipped on my ice-cold Coke, I basked in the sun and once again enjoyed the comfort of warm weather. Once I was settled in the grass, I rapidly untied my hiking boots and stripped off my socks. My earlier suspicion was confirmed: blisters! I'd ended up with a giant blister on the side of my big toe and another one on the bottom of my foot, right under my toes. I knew once I took my boots off that there would be no way my feet would go back in those boots. Throughout the entire hike, I'd never opened my first aid kit, and now that we were done, I finally needed my blister bandages! I was glad it had finally gotten some use. Otherwise, my first aid kit would have ended up being one of those things I'd packed and didn't use. However, better safe than sorry! I'm sure had I not had my first aid kit, there would have been a stronger need for it. It's like the principle of carrying an umbrella when rain is in the forecast. If you don't bring it, it will pour. We waited about an hour and a half total for the rest of the group to join us at the entrance, and many people started drinking beer in celebration. Speaking of celebration, it was time to get the party started!

TIME TO PARTY

WITH THE HIKE OFFICIALLY concluded, we finished the same way we'd started: dancing and singing! Our group of over sixty porters and guides serenaded us with the many songs that had become part of our journey. We danced. We laughed. And we thanked our crew for all their hard work. We could not have survived the hike without them. To think that they do this for a living is absolutely mind-blowing to me. They don't get enough praise for the hardships they go through just to provide for their families. I gained a newfound appreciation for the men and women who literally get paid to climb a mountain and carry other people's shit.

As with our earlier adventures in Africa, it was time for yet another long, hot bus ride. There were many thoughts on my mind as we inched toward the hotel: "Will my luggage make it this time? Will there be hot water to shower?" The quick answer: kind of. I started tracking the location of my luggage to see how far away we were and how long it would take us to get to the hotel. As we got closer to my luggage's location, I got excited. The last time I'd tracked my luggage, it had been left in the US, so you can imagine how much better I felt this time around. We would only be spending one more night in Tanzania and had to share rooms. Team America decided to room together since we had devices with the same plug types (there were three of us on the trip from the US). In fact, our group came from all over the world, including the US, Canada, Poland, the United Kingdom, the Netherlands, Japan, Australia, and Luxembourg.

The only problem with having three people in a room was sharing the shower. Of course, everyone wanted to shower and start getting ready for dinner and a fun night ahead. I let my friends shower first because I don't really take long to get ready. That was a mistake. Unfortunately, there was no hot water by the time I took a shower, and after six days without a shower, my dreams of a hot shower were instantly crushed and would have to wait. At a certain point, you stop caring about the conditions that are unfamiliar to you. Did I want a cold shower? No. But did I want to scrub myself after my longest stretch in my life without a shower? Abso-fucking-lutely.

Finally clean after a week of filth, we got ready! We actually made a pit stop on the way to the hotel to get Kilimanjaro souvenirs that were more affordable than those in the shops that surrounded the mountain, a hack offered up by our guides. I purchased a purple dress with an elephant design, and it felt like the perfect dress to celebrate conquering Africa's tallest point. I straightened my hair, put on some makeup, and made my way to the courtyard for the celebration.

Dinner was a buffet of BBQ, which I was so delighted for. Especially the potatoes! There was a live band playing music, and it was great background ambiance as we all sat together drinking and indulging in a freshly prepared meal. After settling in, we had an informal ceremony acknowledging everyone for reaching the summit. Each person was presented with a certificate that included their name, age, and day/time the summit had been reached. I now have that certificate hanging in my office. It's a memento I will forever cherish.

Afterward, the real party began! When the live music ended and the DJ started playing music, our group got up from their seats and danced and danced and danced. It was such a fun evening celebrating our newfound accomplishment with a group who will forever have a unique bond. We entered the hike as strangers, and we left as friends. As the evening grew later, I got more exhausted and I wasn't able to keep up. Around 11:00 p.m., I decided to venture off to my room. As if I hadn't encountered enough obstacles on this trip, there would be one more … trip, that is. That's right. As I was walking back to my room, it was fairly dark, and I was trying to take a shortcut through the courtyard, and I failed to notice a step down, so I came tumbling down. I caught myself, but only to find out I was breaking my fall with a thorn bush. My hand and foot were instantly covered in thorns. It was so embarrassing, but luckily, no one was around to witness this epic disaster. Once I got back to my room, I immediately saw how swollen my hand was, and I counted my seventeen new splinters. I wanted sleep, but now I needed to perform "surgery" on my hand to get the thorns out. I spent a solid thirty minutes removing as many thorns as possible with my hands, but I needed tweezers. I soaked it in some water as well. Eventually, sleep was more important, so I gave in to that instead.

BEYOND THE
MOUNTAIN

REMEMBER HOW I MENTIONED that climbing Kilimanjaro was only part of the journey? The real challenge went beyond summiting the mountain. Our group had collectively raised over 100,000 euros to support marginalized young women in Kenya. After much-needed celebrations and well-deserved relaxation, our team ventured to Kenya.

We packed our bags and loaded the bus for the four-to-six-hour journey to Nairobi. It was another hot and uncomfortable ride. At the border, we had to exit the bus with all our belongings, go through customs, and then board a new bus. This was a peculiar process, likely a measure to prevent smuggling. One memorable moment was missing our photographer, who was supposed to meet us to get on the bus for Kenya but had been delayed and had to catch up with us there instead.

Upon arriving at the hotel in Kenya, we were welcomed with Wi-Fi and warm showers—not hot, but not freezing, which was a win. There was also a laundry room on-site, so we quickly did a load of laundry to have clean socks, under-garments, and other overworn items. As I finally lay down to relax, I found myself draining fluid from the blisters I had gotten on the final day of the hike. I had only brought hiking boots, camp sandals, and one other pair of sandals. Unfortu-nately, our site visit the next day required closed-toe shoes, so I had to wear my hiking boots again. This was uncomfort-able due to my blisters and the heat. Wearing hiking boots in ninety-degree weather, walking on blacktop, and wearing hiking socks was not ideal—in fact, it was quite painful. But, with no other options, I sucked it up and dealt with it.

Our visit to the communities our funds supported was incredibly impactful and eye-opening. It revealed the stark contrast in living conditions and reminded us of the im-portance of our efforts. This experience, coupled with our climb, truly underscored the significance of resilience and perseverance.

Our first visit in Kenya took us to a local education cen-ter in the village of Kibera, the largest slum in Africa. We began with an icebreaker game that I now love and use for client meetings and introductions. We all stood in a big cir-cle and said, "Hi, my name is ____. I like _____, and I look like _____." The objective was to say you looked like whatever you liked, which made it quite entertaining. For example, a tall person said he liked giraffes and looked like a giraffe, while I said I liked glitter and looked like glitter. It may seem silly, but it was certainly memorable.

After our introduction game, we participated in a mini seminar where we learned about the youth involved in the program and heard about their activities within it. Following the seminar, we split into two large groups for a small field trip. My group visited an internet café, where people paid to use the internet or play video games. We also visited some recycling buyback centers and walked through the village where these youth lived.

During our walk through the village, we had one-on-one conversations with the youth, learning more about their personal lives. This was my first time visiting a third-world country, and seeing these conditions was incredibly eye-opening. It made me truly appreciate what we often take for granted at home. For instance, most homes in the village were made of bricks and had tin roofs, and each one was roughly the size of a traditional bedroom in a standard US home. There was no running water in any of the homes; residents had to walk to a water center and pay for buckets of water. Electricity was limited as well. Even more shocking, none of the homes had bathrooms. Residents had to walk to a public location and pay to use the bathroom, which closed after 10:00 p.m. If they needed to go in the middle of the night, they had no choice but to go outside. Sometimes, the walk was very long too. We take access to toilets and showers for granted. Here, people not only lacked access but also faced costs, time restrictions, and long walks just to use basic facilities. What resonated with me the most, however, was that despite the tough conditions and struggles, they were so full of life and happiness.

This visit was a poignant reminder of the challenging realities many people face daily, underscoring the vital impact of our support and the significance of our fundraising efforts.

As we continued our journey throughout the day, we enjoyed a catered lunch featuring some local cuisine. After lunch, we were divided into groups and informed that we would be playing soccer. We took a long walk to a local soccer field. It was extremely hot outside, and I was wearing my hiking boots as my only option. The field was turf, and it felt like it was burning my feet through my shoes. We waited for a long time, expecting a soccer ball to appear, but it never did. This was where the creativity of the youth shone. They used their imaginations to come up with alternative games for us.

We started by identifying logos from a piece of paper representing large companies, which was a fun challenge. Then, we moved on to more team-building games. In one game, they would give us a letter, and we'd have to quickly form the shape using our bodies. It was a lot of fun, and it was fascinating to see everyone's different ways of thinking. We continued with a few more games throughout the afternoon, and it was finally time to wrap up our day.

After such long, exhausting, but impactful days, the downtime at the hotel quickly became what I looked forward to the most. The chance to relax and reflect on our experiences was invaluable.

The next day, we took another field visit to a dump site and recycling center. As expected, the dump site smelled horrible, with workers required to wear PPE as they sorted through the recyclables. Surprisingly, visiting the recycling center turned out to be incredibly educational. I learned about numerous categories of plastics that I'd previously not known existed. It was fascinating to see how plastics are shredded into small pellets and then resold to generate income.

Overall, the two days of site visits were highly insightful. I'm grateful we had the opportunity to meet the youth, hear their stories, and truly understand the impact of the donations we'd raised. It gives me a great sense of fulfillment knowing that I was part of this initiative.

Aside from the site visits, we had some general downtime and visited a shopping mall as a group. I particularly enjoyed exploring the pharmacies, where you could get medication without a prescription and at a much lower cost than in the United States. It was intriguing to see the different labels and options available. One evening, my friend and I visited a food hall in Nairobi, which offered excellent food and drink selections and was alive with music and dancing. As the journey came to an end, there was one final required adventure before heading back to the States!

AFRICAN SAFARI

DID YOU THINK I could venture to this region of Africa and not go on a safari? Please! If you ever find yourself in Tanzania or Kenya, I highly recommend you carve out some time for a safari. For fans of *The Lion King*, it truly brings the magic of the movie to life right before your eyes.

The group of colleagues who'd summited Kilimanjaro with me went on a three-day safari in the popular Masai Mara area. However, my friend Zuri and I opted for a one-day safari in Nairobi National Park. This was much more cost-friendly at around eighty dollars compared to the five hundred dollars for the three-day adventure. After being away for over ten days, the last thing I wanted was to go camping and spend more time away from showers, beds, and good food. Plus, I didn't want to spend more money as this was already the most expensive trip of my life! Between flights, the tour guide, and supplies required, my total costs landed around $4,500 (or $5,500 if you include my donation contributions).

Our half-day safari started quite literally at the crack of dawn, but it was worth it to see the sun rising over the beautiful landscape. Early morning is also the best time to spot animals. One disclaimer about the Nairobi National Park safari is that you won't see elephants unless you visit the nearby elephant orphanage separately. Otherwise, we got to see most of the other animals.

I was pleased to find out that our safari van would only have me and Zuri on board. This was great because we didn't have to worry about others getting in the way of photo opportunities. Although we stayed in the vehicle the entire time, we were able to stick our heads out of the sunroof area. Seeing the lions up close was a highlight! We even witnessed them mating, which was quite a spectacle.

One moment took us all by surprise, and I'm not making this up. We got the storybook moment! A rhinoceros charged toward our safari van, and I felt like we were about to face a stampede. At the very last second, it turned away. It was so exhilarating and a moment I will never forget! We also saw plenty of zebras, giraffes, crocodiles, warthogs, ostriches, and gazelles. Unfortunately, we didn't spot any leopards or cheetahs; the kitties were apparently sleepy that morning. Ironically, I'd worn leopard-print pants on the safari, so I guess there was a leopard after all.

An African safari truly capped the trip on another high and checked off a new experience from my bucket list. From climbing Kilimanjaro to visiting the largest slum, volunteering, and experiencing a safari, it was finally time to go home.

This journey had been transformative, filled with memories and lessons that would stay with me forever.

LOOKING BACK

I HOPE YOU'VE ENJOYED learning about my Kilimanjaro journey and the adventures beyond it. I'm sure you still have questions, and the most common one I received upon returning was, "Did you have fun?" My candid response was, "Fuck no. Absolutely not." Pardon my French, but this was not a fun trip, nor was it a vacation. This was an opportunity to experience something extraordinary, something most people never do. It was a profound challenge. Would I do it again? Absolutely not. Am I proud of myself? *Hell yes.*

I'm not trying to discourage anyone from climbing Kilimanjaro. In fact, I think everyone should consider it. It's an amazing, once-in-a-lifetime experience. But fun is the last word I would use to describe it. So, for the love of God, stop asking if it was fun. I forgive you if you fell into that category. It's not your fault; it's just a natural question to ask.

Climbing Kilimanjaro will be a memory I hold on to for the rest of my life. It taught me many things, including how I define certain words like tired, sore, hungry, and thirsty.

After experiencing the sleep deprivation leading up to summit night, I now reflect on the word tired any time I use it. Sure, I still say I'm tired from time to time, but when I really think about it, I don't believe I can ever be more tired than I was while climbing that mountain. There's just something about losing oxygen levels and lack of sleep that enhances tiredness to an almost surreal level.

I often ask myself the question, "What would I have done differently?" Should I have prepared better? Should I have brought certain things that I'd omitted? The simple answer is yes. Looking back, I wish I had spent more time climbing hills with a fully stocked backpack to build stronger back muscles and make carrying the bag more bearable. I might have brought different water enhancers to give me something to look forward to, as I disliked the limited beverage options. I most definitely would have brought warmer gear to sleep in at night, and additional layers for summit night, including glove liners and a fleece-lined gaiter.

While I have thoughts of "I wish I did this" or "I wish I did that," at the end of the day, my experience unfolded as it was meant to. I learned a lot along the way. I experienced new emotions and fought mental battles every minute of every day. I made amazing friendships, and I conquered the challenge. The sense of this accomplishment is something I will carry with me forever.

Beyond the physical and mental trials, this journey was a deeply emotional and transformative experience. Climbing Kilimanjaro was not just about reaching the summit; it was about pushing myself beyond my perceived limits, discovering my resilience, and embracing the power of perseverance. Every step, every breath, and every moment of doubt was a test of my strength, both physically and mentally.

This expedition was more than just a climb; it was a journey of self-discovery and growth. I realized the importance of mental fortitude, the value of camaraderie, and the significance of setting ambitious goals. The friendships I forged during this adventure were invaluable, as we supported and motivated each other through every challenge.

The lessons learned from this experience extend beyond the mountain. I now approach life's challenges with a renewed perspective, understanding that true growth often comes from stepping outside of our comfort zones. Climbing Kilimanjaro taught me that I am capable of achieving greatness, even in the face of adversity.

As I reflect on this incredible journey, I am filled with a sense of pride and gratitude. Climbing Kilimanjaro was not just a physical achievement but a testament to the power of determination and the human spirit. It was a journey that tested my limits, transformed my perspective, and left an indelible mark on my soul. And, while I may never embark on such a daunting adventure again, I will always cherish the memories and lessons from this once-in-a-lifetime experience. I did the damn thing!

THE PACKING LIST

IF YOU'RE PREPPING FOR Kilimanjaro, here's everything I had on my packing list. I'll also include the overview of what I wish I had packed, and I'll let you know what things I packed and never used—or packed too much or too little of!

My Original List

- ❏ Hiking boots
- ❏ Camp shoes (slides)
- ❏ Six pairs of hiking socks
- ❏ Two pairs of wool socks
- ❏ Long-sleeve thermal shirt
- ❏ Thermal underwear
- ❏ Underwear (yes, make sure it's on the list)
- ❏ Fleece pullover
- ❏ Rain jacket
- ❏ Beanie (I brought three, and I was so thankful I did)
- ❏ Windproof sunhat

- ❏ Neck gaiter
- ❏ Sunglasses
- ❏ Headlamp
- ❏ Hand warmers
- ❏ Empty water bottles
- ❏ Hydration pack (CamelBak)
- ❏ Sunscreen
- ❏ Lip balm and Vaseline
- ❏ Flushable wipes
- ❏ Toothbrush
- ❏ Toothpaste
- ❏ Floss picks
- ❏ Hand sanitizer
- ❏ Deodorant
- ❏ Tampons and panty liners (ladies, always be prepared!)
- ❏ Body cleansing wipes
- ❏ GoPro
- ❏ Solar charger
- ❏ Portable chargers (I brought five, which was probably overkill)
- ❏ Charging cords
- ❏ iPhone
- ❏ Apple Watch
- ❏ Sleeping bag
- ❏ Snacks
- ❏ Meat protein sticks
- ❏ Candy
- ❏ Goldfish (I wish I had more!)

- ❏ Memory-foam travel pillow
- ❏ Inflatable airplane pillow
- ❏ Journal and pen
- ❏ Hair ties
- ❏ Mini brush
- ❏ Shampoo and conditioner (for after the hike)
- ❏ Medication and vitamins
  - ❏ Pepto-Bismol
  - ❏ Gas-X
  - ❏ Ibuprofen
  - ❏ Fish oil
  - ❏ Joint mobility
  - ❏ Multivitamin
  - ❏ Probiotics
  - ❏ Diamox (to prevent altitude sickness)
- ❏ Hydration sticks
- ❏ Protein powder

Original-List Items I Didn't Use

- ❏ Extra AAA batteries
- ❏ Quick-dry towel
- ❏ GoGirl device (this allows women to pee standing up)
- ❏ Dry shampoo
- ❏ Bug spray
- ❏ First aid kit (fortunately, I only needed this after the hike)

❑ Antimalarial pills (the guides told us not to take them)

What I Wish I'd Packed

❑ Fuzzy socks (for bedtime)
❑ Fleece balaclava
❑ Nail clippers
❑ Gum
❑ More warm layers (for bedtime)
❑ Fleece sleeping bag insert
❑ More snacks!
❑ Juice boxes
❑ Rain pants

ABOUT THE AUTHOR

WRITING HAS BEEN A lifelong passion for Danica, a form of expression that often feels like her love language. The idea of conquering Mount Kilimanjaro and penning a book was beyond her wildest dreams, but she embraced both challenges with open arms because she views life as a tapestry of risks and continuous self-improvement. Danica resides in Orlando, Florida.

Join Danica Paige in unraveling more tales of exploration, experiences, and discoveries at https://www. instagram.com/ danicadiscoveries!

www.ingramcontent.com/pod-product-compliance
Lightning Source LLC
Chambersburg PA
CBHW030924140626
46545CB00016B/2347